Creating Flat Design Websites

Design and develop your own flat design websites in HTML

António Pratas

[PACKT] open source*
PUBLISHING
community experience distilled

BIRMINGHAM - MUMBAI

Creating Flat Design Websites

First published: April 2014

Production Reference: 1160414

Published by Packt Publishing Ltd.
Livery Place
35 Livery Street
Birmingham B3 2PB, UK.

ISBN 978-1-78398-004-8

www.packtpub.com

Cover Image by Faiz Fattohi (faizfattohi@gmail.com)

Credits

Author
António Pratas

Reviewers
Eddy Borja
Pedro Piñera Buendia
Emrullah Lüleci

Commissioning Editor
Rebecca Youé

Acquisition Editor
Rebecca Youé

Content Development Editor
Priyanka Shah

Technical Editors
Mrunal Chavan
Edwin Moses

Copy Editors
Sayanee Mukherjee
Karuna Narayanan
Alfida Paiva
Adithi Shetty

Project Coordinators
Melita Lobo
Akash Poojary

Proofreader
Simran Bhogal

Indexer
Priya Subramani

Production Coordinator
Arvindkumar Gupta

Cover Work
Arvindkumar Gupta

About the Author

António Pratas is a Portuguese designer living in London. He has an MSc in Multimedia Design and has been working as a designer since 2005. He has worked with advertising agencies and in design ateliers, including Euro RSCG (now Havas), Bürocratik, and Universidade de Coimbra. He has also co-founded a small design atelier and a web startup. He previously wrote articles for `designmodo.com`, `webdesignerdepot.com`, and `awwwards.com`.

Acknowledgment

I always looked up to good and famous designers/authors as if they had the answers to all design problems. However, eventually I found out that design is not about the answers, it's about asking the right questions, and even these great designers are, in the end, only humans. There's no correct way or formula on how to do things or solve problems, it's about choosing a path and trusting you're doing what is best for each problem you're faced with.

This book would not have been possible without the support of my lovely girlfriend Márcia Gaudêncio. Thank you for all your help and patience, and for all the meals you cooked and chores you've done that should've been my responsibility, while I was busy with my laptop for hours on end.

I'd also like to thank Rebecca Youé for offering me the chance of writing my first book, as well as the Packt Publishing team and reviewers for their great work in reviewing and helping out over and over again.

Last but (definitely) not least, I'd like to thank my father, António Redondo Pratas, and my mother, Leopoldina Correia for giving me all they could ever give me, making me everything that I am today, and teaching me all that I know and do. You can't find these things in any book. Obrigado!

About the Reviewers

Eddy Borja has witnessed the evolution of websites from their static Web 1.0 beginnings to the modern designs that we have now, throughout his life. His first exposure to web design and development began during his teenage years, and he has been involved in the creation of web and mobile apps ever since. He has been a consultant for many startups and a co-founder of a software development shop that builds mobile apps for its clients.

As always, I'd like to thank my parents and my family for their never-ending support, and my love, Karla Salazar, for her support and encouragement.

Pedro Piñera Buendia is an Electronics and Telecommunication engineer from Spain. He started working as a mobile developer in 2010, and since then, he has been involved in developing applications that are related to health and entertainment. He is currently working as an iOS developer for Redbooth, a platform to help companies manage their projects (through tasks, notes, conversations, and so on).

I would like to thank my girlfriend and Merengue (my dog) for waiting for me while I was helping the author review this book.

Emrullah Lüleci is an entrepreneur, a software engineer, and a UX designer. He has been developing cloud-based Android and web applications. He believes in the power of open source. Thus, he owns several open source projects and contributes to many others. Even though his background is based on programming, he is passionate about designing and creating unique interfaces, which are mainly flat. He is also a member of several communities and delivers speeches about mobile app designs and their development. Emrullah is the founder of CengaLabs, which focuses on developing mobile applications and sharing all the new tools that are created for the projects in open source.

Table of Contents

Preface

Flat design is a digital style of design that has been one of the biggest trends in recent years in web and user interface design. It is famous for its extremely minimalistic style. It has appeared at a time when skeuomorphic, a style of creating realistic interfaces, was considered to be the biggest and most famous trend, making this a really rough and extreme transition for both users and designers.

Creating Flat Design Websites will explain the story of flat design since its early roots to the present day, while also showing you some of the most famous examples and explaining how to design and implement your own flat design website in a practical and easy way.

What this book covers

Chapter 1, What is Flat Design?, explains what flat design is, its history since the introduction of the international typographic style, and how it has evolved over the years. We will also understand what brands helped bring the flat design to light and how this style became more evident as a trend for more brands and interfaces, such as the recently released iOS 7 from Apple.

Chapter 2, Designing in Flat, covers how to design in flat and what are the most important things that the designer should have in mind while designing. It will focus on the importance of typography, alignment, and creating a layout by always using a clear, invisible grid and creating more predictable layouts.

Chapter 3, Creating a Flat and Usable Interface, shows why you should focus on web usability and how important it is for the good functioning of flat design websites. The main focus is to avoid any kind of damage to the interface, its navigation and readability to exemplify this, we will create some tests and visual exercises.

Chapter 4, Designing Your Own Flat Website, will show you, step-by-step, how to design your single page flat website. We will cover the entire journey from planning visual sections to deciding on layout and navigation, up to the final pixels.

Chapter 5, Developing Your Site, will explain how to develop the page designed in the previous chapter using Designmodo flat UI Bootstrap components. We will cover how to code the basic static page, as well as jQuery transitions and CSS3 effects.

Chapter 6, Creating Your Own Flat UI Kit, will go over the creation of your own kit while reviewing all the work that you have done. We will see how to organize our images, styles, and effects, and save them for future usage as a personal Flat UI kit.

What you need for this book

Throughout this book, we will be creating a design of a web page and develop some code, specifically HTML, CSS, and JavaScript (with the help of jQuery). For the design, we will be using Photoshop, and any version from CS4 onwards will suffice. For the code, we will require a code editor such as Sublime Text, which may be downloaded and evaluated for free from `http://sublimetext.com`; it's a great piece of software. You can also use any other code editor of your preference, such as Notepad++ for Windows (`http://notepad-plus-plus.org/`), Coda (`http://panic.com/coda/`)for Linux, or Espresso (`http://macrabbit.com/espresso/`) for Mac.

Who this book is for

This book is for designers and developers who are interested in creating websites. Ideally, you should have some prior knowledge of design notions, but it is essential to know how to use Photoshop at a beginner/medium level. This is also written for designers who already have some knowledge on frontend development, as we will develop a website using HTML, CSS, and JavaScript (with the help of jQuery).

Conventions

In this book, you will find a number of styles of text that distinguish between different kinds of information. Here are some examples of these styles, and an explanation of their meaning.

Code words in text, database table names, folder names, filenames, file extensions, pathnames, dummy URLs, user input, and Twitter handles are shown as follows: "We will now create the styles for our `<body>` element."

A block of code is set as follows:

```
<!DOCTYPE html>
<html lang="en">
<head>
</head>
<body>
<button class="btn">Click Here</button>
</body>
</html>
```

New terms and **important words** are shown in bold. Words that you see on the screen, in menus or dialog boxes for example, appear in the text like this: "Clicking the **Next** button moves you to the next screen."

[Warnings or important notes appear in a box like this.]

[Tips and tricks appear like this.]

Reader feedback

Feedback from our readers is always welcome. Let us know what you think about this book—what you liked or may have disliked. Reader feedback is important for us to develop titles that you really get the most out of.

To send us general feedback, simply send an e-mail to `feedback@packtpub.com`, and mention the book title via the subject of your message.

If there is a topic that you have expertise in and you are interested in either writing or contributing to a book, see our author guide on `www.packtpub.com/authors`.

Customer support

Now that you are the proud owner of a Packt book, we have a number of things to help you to get the most from your purchase.

Downloading the example code

You can download the example code files for all Packt books you have purchased from your account at `http://www.packtpub.com`. If you purchased this book elsewhere, you can visit `http://www.packtpub.com/support` and register to have the files e-mailed directly to you.

Errata

Although we have taken every care to ensure the accuracy of our content, mistakes do happen. If you find a mistake in one of our books—maybe a mistake in the text or the code—we would be grateful if you would report this to us. By doing so, you can save other readers from frustration and help us improve subsequent versions of this book. If you find any errata, please report them by visiting `http://www.packtpub.com/submit-errata`, selecting your book, clicking on the **errata submission form** link, and entering the details of your errata. Once your errata are verified, your submission will be accepted and the errata will be uploaded on our website, or added to any list of existing errata, under the Errata section of that title. Any existing errata can be viewed by selecting your title from `http://www.packtpub.com/support`.

Piracy

Piracy of copyright material on the Internet is an ongoing problem across all media. At Packt, we take the protection of our copyright and licenses very seriously. If you come across any illegal copies of our works, in any form, on the Internet, please provide us with the location address or website name immediately so that we can pursue a remedy.

Please contact us at `copyright@packtpub.com` with a link to the suspected pirated material.

We appreciate your help in protecting our authors, and our ability to bring you valuable content.

Questions

You can contact us at `questions@packtpub.com` if you are having a problem with any aspect of the book, and we will do our best to address it.

1
What is Flat Design?

In this chapter, what flat design is and how this style came to be will be explained. We will cover its predecessors in graphic design since 1950, moving on to how important skeuomorphic design was in the process of making flat design one of the biggest trends in digital design in the last few years.

We will also learn what the current status of flat design is, how it has been adopted by some of the biggest brands in the market, and how we interact everyday with interfaces designed in flat design. There's also a simple exercise to help you understand how to build a skeuomorphic element and its flat counterpart, to better clarify the differences between skeuomorphic and flat design.

Defining flat design

Flat design is a digital design style that was one of the most discussed trends throughout 2013. It is characterized by a really minimalistic look, focused on removing all extra elements and effects from a design, such as bevels, shadows, lighting effects, depth, texture, and every element that creates and gives an extra dimension to these elements.

This kind of treatment results in creating a very simple and clean look that seems visually flat on the screen, by using white space, bright colors, and simple lines as layout elements. Flat design, as a style, rose quickly to fame and to mass use because of its impactful look but surprisingly simple approach. It started to gather a big fan base and supporters of the style, because most people saw in flat design an opportunity for them to be able to create a simple and good looking web page.

It was undoubtedly one of the most discussed topics in design during 2013, and as there were many supporters, there were also a large number of people opposed to such a style and against the importance and discussion of it.

Also, one of the biggest reasons why flat design was so impactful in the community was because of its timing. Flat design came in a time when skeuomorphic design was one of the most famous and used styles in digital design and interfaces. They contrasted in such a significant way that it was indeed a really rough and extreme transition for users of these apps as well as for designers that needed to switch their design style to accommodate the users' wishes and expectations. And what is skeuomorphic design, you say?

History and evolution

Flat design as a digital design trend and name surfaced on the web around 2012. As a response and alternative to skeuomorphic designs, the first adopters got a lot of attention because it was considered a risk to go down a path of creating such simple and clear layouts, opposed to the complex and heavy ones being created at the time. This shift of trends is something that always happened, as history shows. Fashion and style are cyclic, and in this day and age where everything is digital, these cycles tend to be even shorter and changes can happen quicker than ever.

To truly find the first origins of flat, we need to go back to 1950, with the development of the International Typographic Style (or the Swiss Style). This style was also focused on creating a clean, readable design in contrast to the complex illustrations, textures, and photos used in printed posters at the time. It was also when Akzidenz-Grotesk, the first version of the typeface that would eventually become Helvetica, started to be used more often, which gave a newfound strength and focus on sans-serif typography. Typography was one of the big focus points of the posters of the Swiss Style, specifically big sans-serif type, thus creating a really impactful message. We can say that this is historically the first form of flat design.

Some decades later, already in the digital spectrum, Microsoft was one of those responsible for pushing this kind of minimalistic look forward with the launch of the Zune music player in 2006. Even though the device in itself wasn't a commercial success, its interface was revolutionary. The focus on thin and big typography, and its clear and minimalistic approach to its navigation and iconography, was one of the roots for today's Microsoft interfaces redesign, which can still be found on the strongly typographic menus presented on the Windows Phone. Zune also influenced other products, such as the Xbox 360 dashboard and Windows 8. The Windows 8 interface, known by the code name **Metro UI**, was also one of the biggest interface overhauls that emphasized the flat design style. It was a great change of look for Microsoft Windows and a really bold one that generated a lot of appraisal by the design community and influenced a lot of websites that try to replicate the squared layout up to this day. The following screenshot shows the use of flat design in Metro UI:

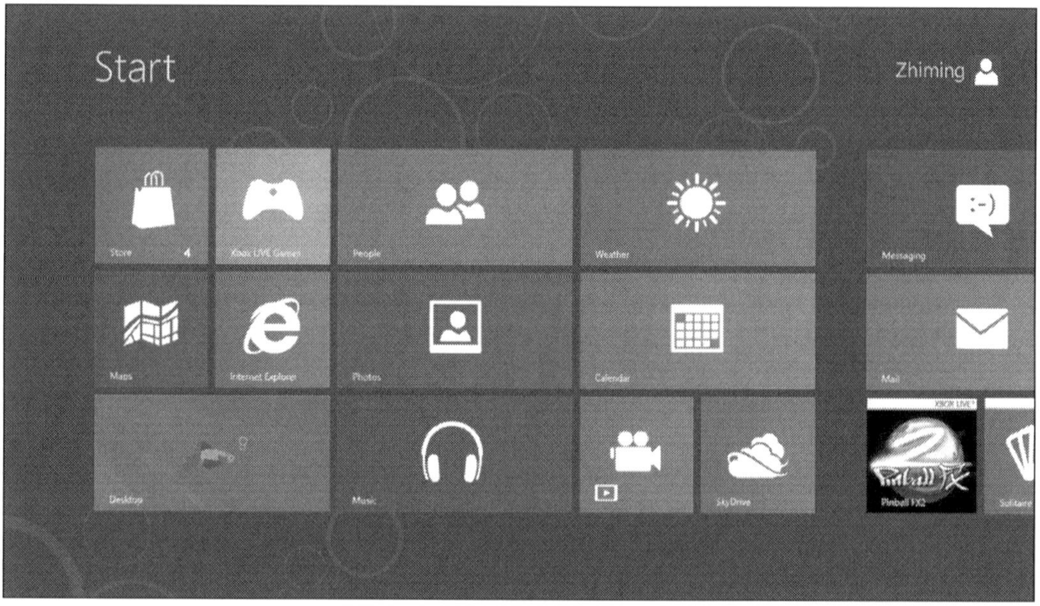

But getting back to the definition of flat design, this as a term and as a style was defined by designers who wrote about this subject. One of them, Allan Grinshtein, from LayerVault—a version control for designers—wrote in his post *The Flat Design Era* (`http://layervault.tumblr.com/post/32267022219/flat-interface-design`) how he believes that *elegant interfaces are ones that have the most impact with the fewest elements*. This, along with the success and great feedback on the LayerVault flat design interface, reinforced the notion that a very minimalistic interface can be thought out to be usable and achieve great success among an application's user base. At this time, and with the success of the first bold designers, the community followed and adhered to this style, creating an enormous number of design proposals and applications following the flat design aesthetic.

Skeuomorphic versus flat

Skeuomorphic design, also known as realism, is a style that was very much used during 2012 and 2013, and it consists of creating visual elements that represent their original, physical counterpart.

Skeuomorphism is defined as an element of design or structure that serves little or no purpose in the artifact fashioned from the new material but was essential to the object made from the original material (*courtesy: Wikipedia*—`http://en.wikipedia.org/wiki/Skeuomorph`).

Apple created several skeuomorphic interfaces for their desktop and mobile apps; apps such as iCal, iBooks, Find My Friends, Podcast apps, and several others.

This kind of interface was both loved and hated among the design community and users. It was a style that focused a lot on the detail and texture, making the interface heavier and often more complex, but interesting because of the clear connection to the real objects depicted here. It was an enjoyable and rich experience for the user due to the high detail and interaction that a skeuomorphic interface presented, which served to attract the eye to the detail and care put into these designs; for example, the page flip in iBooks, visually representing the swipe of a page as in a traditional book. But this style also had its downsides.

Besides being a harsh transition from the traditional interfaces (as in the case of Apple, in which it meant coming from its famous glassy and clean looking Aqua interface), several skeuomorphic applications on the desktop didn't seem to fit in the overall OS look. Apart from stylistic preferences and incoherent looks, skeuomorphic design is also a bad design choice because the style in itself is a limitation to innovation. By replicating the traditional and analogical designs, the designer doesn't have the option or the freedom to imagine, create, and design new interfaces and interactions with the user. Flat design, being the extremely simple and clear style that it is, gives all the freedom to the designer by ignoring any kind of limitations and effects. But both styles have a place and time to be used, and skeuomorphic is great for applications such as Propellerheads that are directly replacing hardware, such as audio mixers. Using these kinds of interfaces makes it easier for new users to learn how to use the real hardware counterpart, while at the same time previous users of the hardware will already know how to use the interface with ease.

Regardless of the style, a good designer must be ready to create an interface that is adapted to the needs of the user and the market. To exemplify this and to better learn the basic differences between flat and skeuomorphic, let's do a quick exercise.

Exercise 1 – the skeuomorphic and flat buttons

In this exercise, we'll create a simple call to an action button, the copy of *Buy Now*. We'll create this element twice; first we'll take a look at the skeuomorphic approach by creating a realistic looking button with texture, shadow, and depth. Next, we will simply convert it to its flat counterpart by removing all those extra elements and adapting it to a minimalistic style.

You should have all the materials you'll need for this exercise. We will use the typeface Lato, also available for free on Google Fonts, and the image `wood.jpg` for the texture on the skeuomorphic button. We'll just need Photoshop for this exercise, so let's open it up and use the following steps:

1. Create a new Photoshop document with 800 x 600 px. This is where we will create our buttons.
2. Let's start by creating the skeuomorphic one. We start by creating a rectangle with the rounded rectangle tool, with a radius of 20 px. This will be the face of our button. To make it easier to visualize the element while we create it, let's make it gray (`#a2a2a2`).

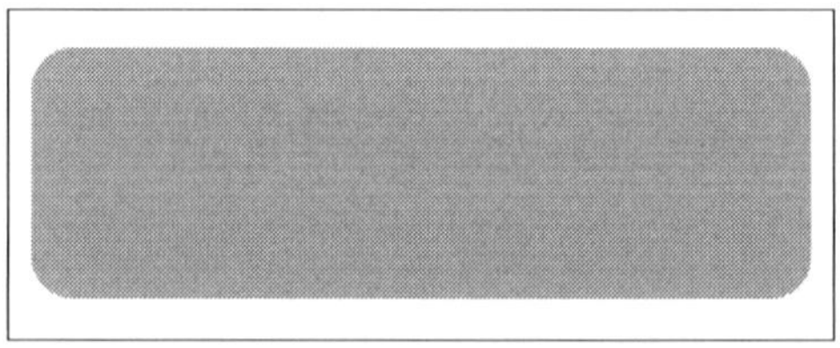

3. Now that we have our button face created, let's give some depth to this button. Just duplicate the layer (*command* + *J* on Mac or *Ctrl* + *J* on Windows) and pull it down to 10 or 15 px, whichever you prefer. Let's make this new rectangle a darker shade of gray (`#393939`) and make sure that this layer is below the face layer. You should now have a simple gray button with some depth. The side layer simulates the depth of the button by being pulled down for just a couple of pixels, and since we made it darker, it resembles a shadow.

4. Now for the call to action. Create a textbox on top of the button face, set its width to that of the button, and center the text. In there, write `Buy Now`, and set the text to Lato, weight to Black, and size to 50 pt. Center it vertically just by looking at the screen, until you find that it sits correctly in the center of the button.

5. Now to make this button really skeuomorphic, let's get our image `wood.jpg`, and let's use it as our texture. Create a new layer named `wood-face` and make sure it's above our `face` layer. Now to define the layer as a texture and use our button as a mask, we're going to right-click on the layer and click on **Create clipping mask**. This will mask our texture to overlay the button face.

6. For the side texture, duplicate the `wood-face` layer, rename it to `wood-side` and repeat the preceding instructions for the side layer. After that, and to have a different look, move the `wood-face` layer around and look for a good area of the texture to use on the side, ideally something with some up strips to make it look more realistic.

7. To finish the side, create a new layer style in the `side` layer, `gradient overlay`, and make a gradient from black to transparent and change the settings as shown in the following screenshot. This will make a shadow effect on top of the wood, making it look a lot better.

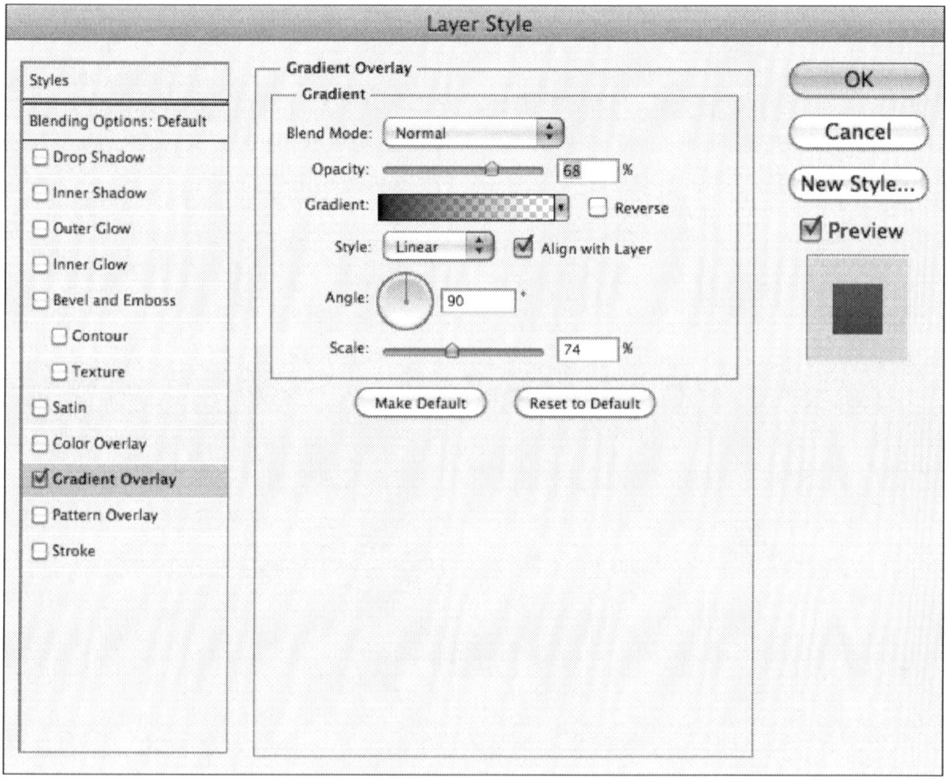

8. To finish our skeuomorphic button, let's go back to the text and define the color as `#7b3201` (or another shade of brown; try to pick from the button and make it slightly darker until you find that it looks good), so that it looks like the text is carved in the wood.

9. The last touch will be to add an **Inner Shadow** layer style in the text with the settings shown. Group all the layers and name it `Skeuomorphic` and we're done.

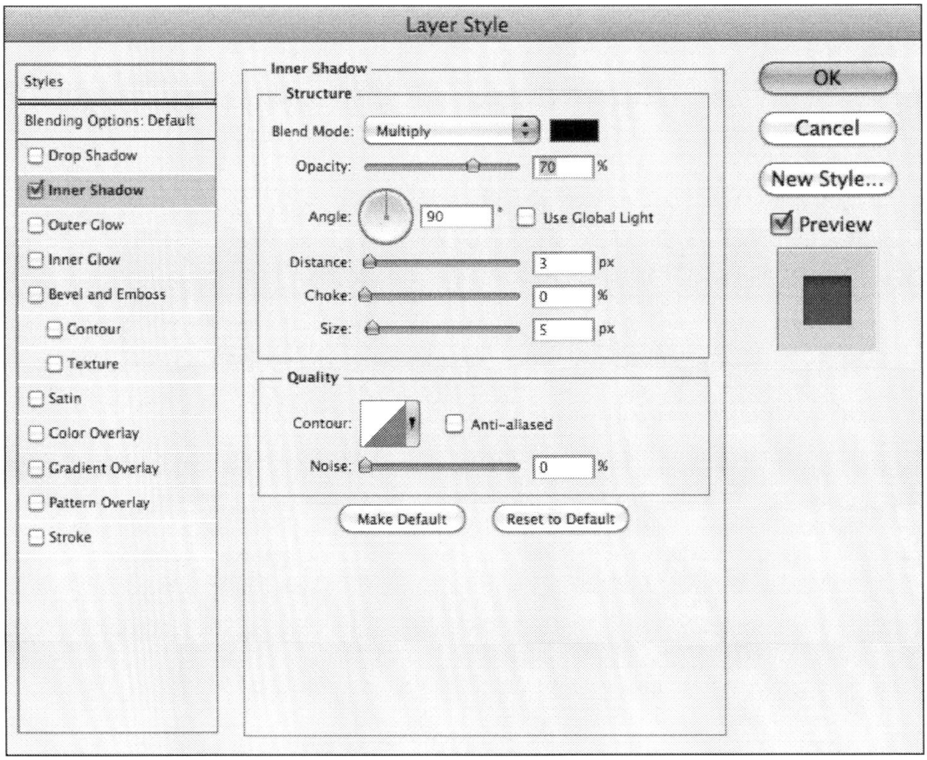

And now we have our skeuomorphic button. It's a really simple way of doing it but we recreated the look of a button made out of wood just by using shapes, texture, and some layer styles.

Now for our flat version:

1. Duplicate the group we just created and name it `flat`. Move it to the other half of the workspace.
2. Delete the following layers: `wood-face`, `wood-side`, and `side`.

3. This button will not have any depth, so we do not need the side layer as well as the textures. To keep the button in the same color scheme as our previous one, we'll use the color `#7b3201` for our text and face. We'll make a transparent button, which only has color on the border and fills up on a mouse hover (we will cover those effects later in the book). Your document should look like what is shown in the following screenshot:

4. Create a new layer style and choose **Stroke** with the following settings. This will create the border of our button. To make the button transparent, let's reduce the **Layer Fill** option to 0 percent, which will leave only the layer styles applied.

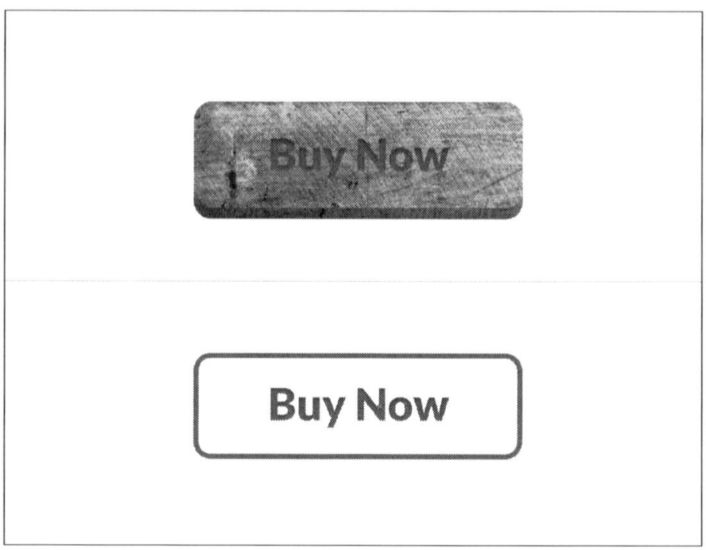

5. Let's remove the layer styles from our text to make it flat, reduce the weight of the font to **Bold** to make it thinner and roughly the same weight of the border, and align it visually, and our flat button is done!

This type of a transparent button is great for flat interfaces, especially when used over a blurred color background. This is because it creates an impactful button with very few elements to it, creating a transparent control and making great use of the white space in the design. In design, especially when designing flat, remember that less is more.

With this exercise, you were able to build a skeuomorphic element and deconstruct it down to its flat version, which is as simple as a rounded rectangle with border and text. The font we chose is frequently used for flat design layouts; it's simple but rounded and it works great with rounded-corner shapes such as the ones we just created.

The use of flat in the real world

There was an incredibly quick adoption and usage from the designers on this style. Big brands and companies such as Apple, Google, and Facebook redesigned their interfaces and brands to create a simpler look. iOS 7, the mobile operating system of the Apple iPhone, is definitely the biggest example of this adoption, since its interface was completely redesigned to simplify the navigation, controls, iconography, and pretty much every element existent in the operating system. This was already expected given the kind of changes seen in the user interface world, but it was an enormous jump from iOS 6 and its skeuomorphic apps to iOS 7 and its flat look and experimental interfaces. A lot more brands followed this transition, such as Facebook, and redesigned their brand and app to be simpler and flatter. Most mobile apps redesigned their interfaces and their icons and adhered to this flat style. Less is more; flat design helped brands understand that and change their look to a simpler and cleaner one. Have a look at the following examples:

- Facebook logo redesign (old version and the new flat redesign):

- Google logo redesign (old version and the new flat redesign):

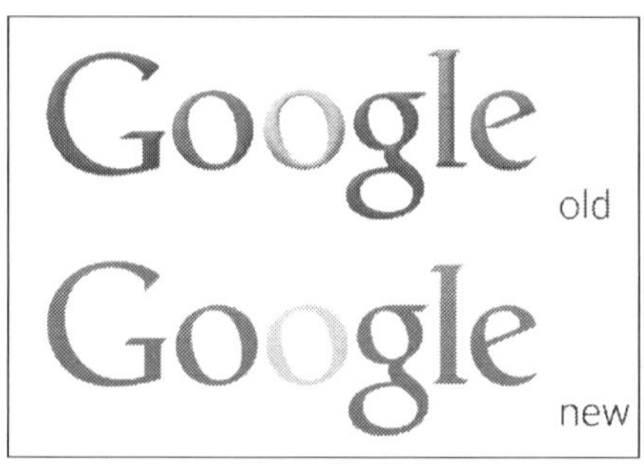

- Apple iOS for the iPhone (on the left, iOS 6 and on the right, iOS 7, redesigned to have a flat look, which can be seen in the icons used):

Summary

So there you have it! We looked at how flat is not new as a design style as its minimalistic look can be traced back to the 1950s with the International Typographic Style. We also covered how to design in skeuomorphic and in flat, and what their main differences are. Also, we learnt how important and how widespread the flat design is over some world famous companies such as Google, Facebook, and Apple, having redesigned their logos and user interfaces to match that look.

Now that we know what flat design is, next we will discover how to design in flat, and what you, as a designer, should focus on to create a great flat interface.

2
Designing in Flat

This chapter covers how to design in flat and what the most important things that you need focus on while designing are. It will also cover the importance of typography, alignment, and grid and layout to create better and more readable designs. Read on to learn all the things to keep in mind while designing in flat, and prepare yourself to start creating your own flat design projects.

Design style

Flat design is a style that, as the name suggests, resembles a flat surface. This look and style rose quickly among designers due to its simplicity while retaining a great impact. In this chapter, we will cover the restrictions and rules of flat design, what you should do and shouldn't do, as well as when to use flat design in your layouts.

A flat design website looks organized, clean, and yet very professional. Imagine a room filled with furniture, tables, couches, rugs, pots, and plants. You have been in a room like that, and even though it feels cozy, it feels cramped and sometimes, with just a bit too much of things. Now imagine removing those tables, couches, and rugs and leaving just the bare essentials: one rug, one couch, and only one small useful table. The white walls will look clearer and bigger, and the room will feel clearer and more spacious. For a designer starting in flat design, such as yourself, this is roughly the same process that you need to go through, by removing all the extra images, details, and effects such as drop shadows and gradients, and just focusing on showing the message with a flat background and flat color.

Flat design is definitely a trend. It's one that is sticking for a long time though, and the reason for that is there's good learning and good interfaces coming out of it. It's really common for designers to follow trends and create their work based on the style that is currently being used more frequently. After all, inspiration comes daily from pretty much everywhere we look, and the Web is something that we're constantly using. New ideas and approaches from designers on layouts create new paradigms and design patterns, and as such, it's just natural that we, as designers, follow these patterns. This leads to a constant improvement of the layouts and new ideas for interfaces, and with flat it is exactly the same. It's a specific style that has a specific look. If you want to create a flat design, you should stick to these kind of rules, and in the end, just get the best out of the style and mix it with your own. These rules can be seen as limitations as well, but that, in design, is not always a bad thing.

Working with limitations

I believe that flat design is not a natural style; it's not something that you'd find yourself using on your own without forcing it. Even the most minimalistic websites don't usually go for a flat look, as flat has its specific look and certain *rules*.

This happens because designers often detect flaws and problems on a design and try to overcome them with embellishments and workarounds. Text that doesn't read well over every image usually has a subtle drop shadow to make sure that there's a darker background to make the text contrast enough to always be readable. These are the challenges that the designer is faced with. These limitations make designing interesting, because by removing all these crutches, the designer finds himself or herself focusing only on what's important.

In an academic context, when a student is given a design project, where they are allowed to design whatever they want and are also able to choose which medium to use as the style, it often ends up with worse results than a student who is given a specific theme and medium. For example, by knowing that you're designing a website for children's toys, you have your focus and objective. When you're allowed to do everything, it's hard to know exactly what you want to focus on. Limitations work great in project management, to make you focus your mind on the most important tasks as well on design. This lets you design the elements that are needed and focus on the style that is more adequate to the objective in mind.

Flat is indeed a style that has its own set of limitations. You need to design something that looks flat and doesn't use any of the usual effects that you'd normally find yourself being able to use. You need to follow a certain aesthetic; it has to be simple, it needs to have a lot of white space, and it has to look structured and organized. The space in which you put your content will have to be very well thought out, as it usually will be a smaller portion. If you have a big page with dozens of text blocks, you end up having a more cramped layout and won't be able to get that aesthetic look you were trying to aim for.

Define your limitations and make your layout as optimized as possible. If a certain copy or image isn't needed, just remove it. The simpler it gets, the clearer it will look in the end.

Flat is not always the answer

As with every style, flat design should be used in websites and products where the look fits the target and objective of the product. Not all websites or apps will benefit from using a flat aesthetic design. A flat design look is, indeed, really flexible and can be used in very different types of markets and targets, but always keep your objective in mind. Use flat only if it makes sense for the project in hand. Each project is different and how you want to convey the message in your website or interact with your users through your user interface varies from project to project.

Flat can be easily used and found in designer portfolios, corporate websites, web apps, mobile apps, restaurants, and a lot of other different examples, but you need to ask yourself this question: is flat a good look for my website? If you're creating a game website, such as a RPG, or promoting a premium and expensive product, such as a watch or a good wine, you're probably better off skipping flat. The reason is that these are projects that will benefit a lot from textures and effects such as gradients and shadows, and allow the designer to create a more premium and subtle look. A game website, for instance, is made up of game images and futuristic or old elements, which are always associated with the game in question. Imagine how boring it would be if the World of Warcraft website is in a flat design. So, make sure that your project is adequate for a flat look and don't just use the style regardless of the objective, as it will defeat the purpose and lose all impact.

The following screenshot shows the *World of Warcraft* website:

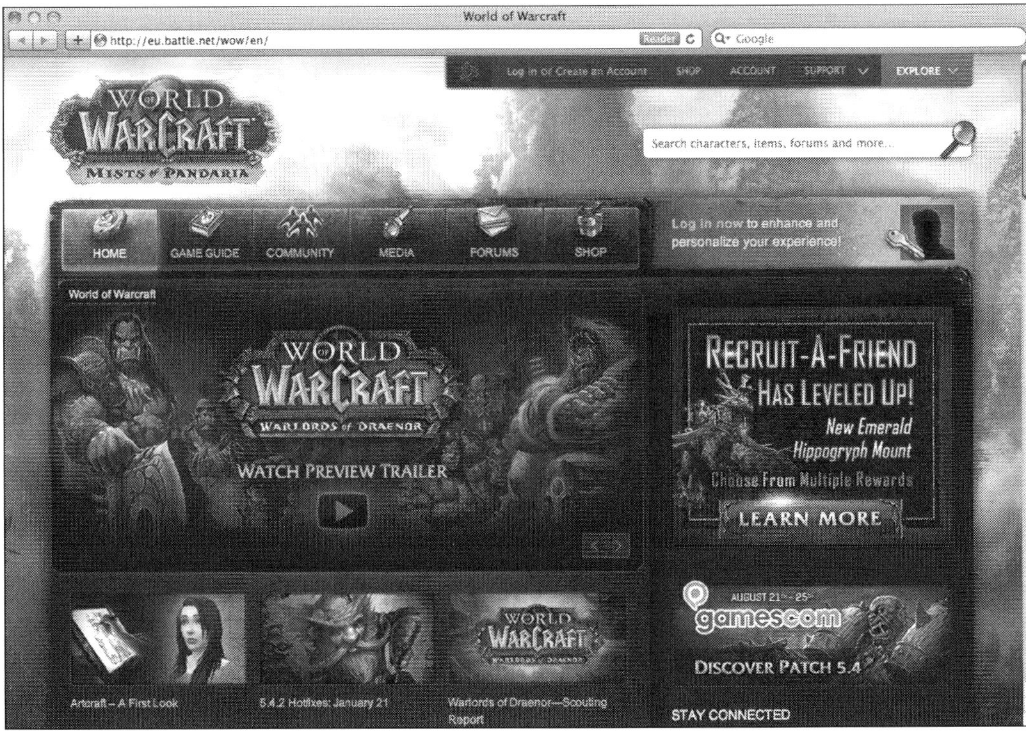

Lose your "crutches"

That's right, flat design has a "no crutches" rule. All drop shadows, bevels, glows, gradients, lighting effects, textures, and embosses should not be used here, as this limitation is the best way to learn and practice creating flat designs.

If you're looking to create a really flat look, you need to make sure that your design is, indeed, flat. However, don't think that flat is a dictatorship; you can always try to create a flat 3D look, which looks really great, and yes, shadows are allowed. Every designer tries to add and improve the style with their own ideas, and great icons come along the way. The use of shadows and lighting shouldn't disrupt the flat look. So, start by designing as flat as possible, focusing on the important things that make flat design look great. The design includes the grid, the white space, the composition, and the typography; when you feel comfortable, try adding these new elements, as they look really good. There's even a style of shadow, called **long shadow**, used with flat. This basically resembles a light close to the ground, creating a heavy and long shadow on the surface. This creates a cool looking effect. Have a look at the following screenshot:

Flat Design Icons Set from Pixeden (left) and the Motorola Long Shadow logo from Sajeer Mohamed (right)

Photos or illustration?

The answer to this question is pretty simple: both.

Flat design illustration is something that was picked up really fast by designers, especially to design flat iconography, thus achieving a very interesting effect using flat colors on these icons. These illustrations look great and are really a good complement to the flat look on your website (if they are indeed relevant to your product and target), but photos can (and should) also be used. Flat is not only about text and simple colors; it's about creating a layout where your photos and your content stands out, by bringing the focus of the user on the content instead of on the interface. This was something that often happened on skeuomorphic interfaces.

Nowadays, it's very common to see websites using very wide and high-resolution photos of people, products, or environment to showcase their product in a real-life situation more easily. It is frequently said that a picture is worth a thousand words, so, use those pictures well to help you communicate your message. Photos can be very important in setting the mood and tone of the website; a flat design looks great over a picture, as it's a mix between the complex (image) and the simple (layout), which gives a great contrast between the two.

If you're looking for some predesigned flat icons, there are several freely available icon sets online, created by designers and for designers.

The following are some examples that you can use in your projects:

- Flat Design Icons Set Vol1 by Pixeden (`http://www.pixeden.com/media-icons/flat-design-icons-set-vol1`)
- Free Flat Icons by buatoom (`http://dribbble.com/shots/1095922-Free-Flat-Icons`)

- Free Flat Icons by Jan Dvořák (http://dribbble.com/shots/1054478-Free-Flat-Icons)
- Flat Icon Collection (http://www.flaticon.com/)
- Flat Icons Collection (http://flaticons.net/)

Flat is great because it is such a simple style that allows you to showcase its content. In the end, it's all about the content, and the design's function is to give that content to the user/reader in the easiest and quickest way. So, use and abuse your pictures while designing in flat; let the content do the talking instead of the interface. The following screenshot is a good example:

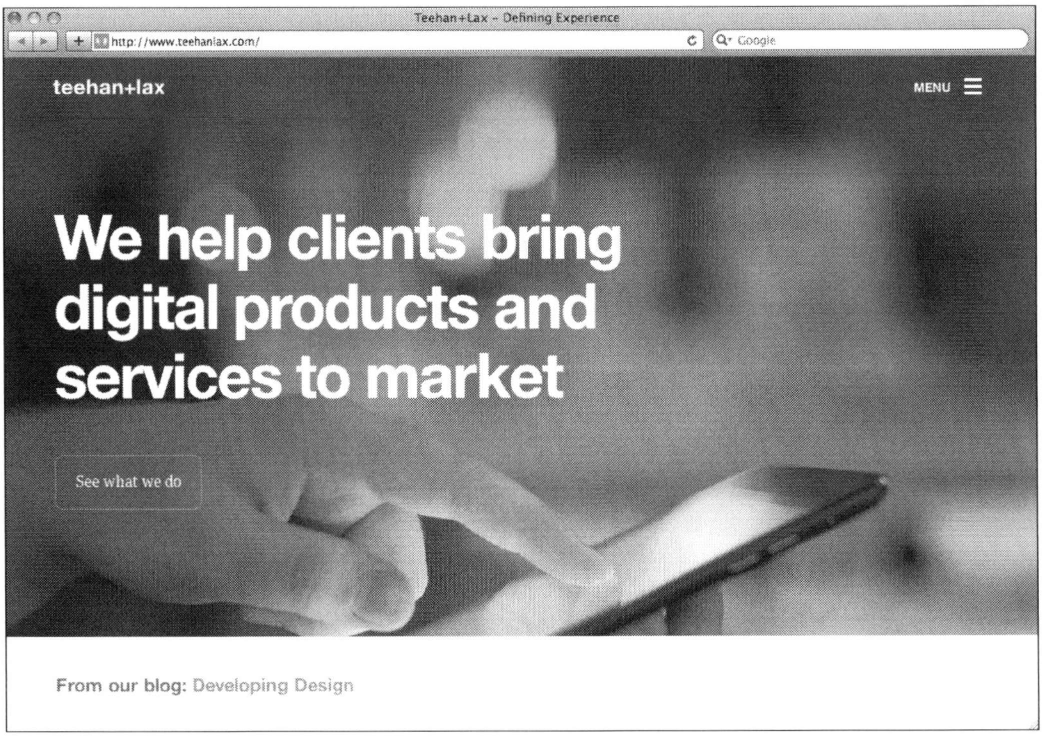

Teehan+Lax design studio homepage

Respecting the grid

Grid is an important tool in graphic design as well as in digital design. The grid is a combination of imaginary lines that define the spacing and dimensions of the main layout and it's the foundation of an interface, on top of which the layout will be designed. It's a framework that gives the user the orientation and guidance to design every page and every content of a section, without having to worry about alignment, safe margins, and spacing. This is because the grid was already developed earlier to avoid these calculations for each page. Have a look at the following screenshot:

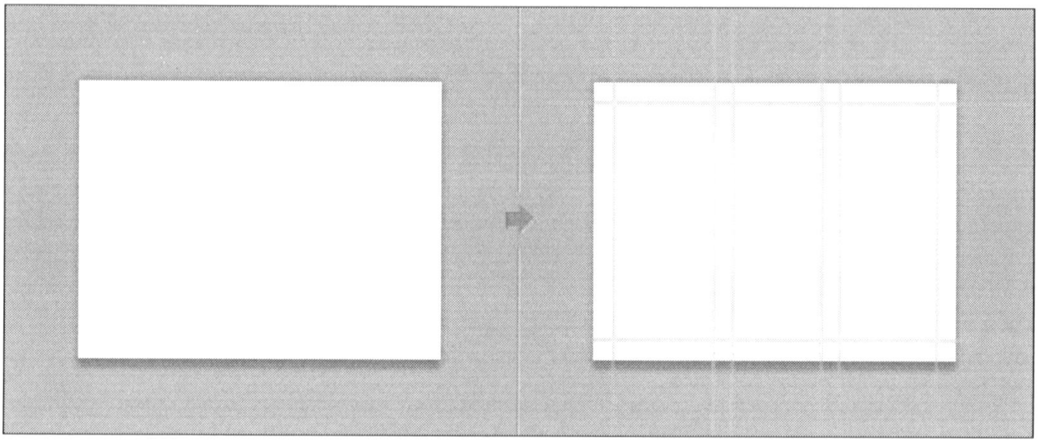

Photoshop guides with the Guide plugin

The grid is definitely essential on every design piece, but its importance is undeniable for flat. Since flat designs tend to have less boxes and lines, the grid is extremely important to hold all the visual elements together to form a layout. Two elements aligned can give the viewer the perception of a block or a line, and these visual perceptions are built using this grid and by ensuring that these alignments are correct.

White space is one of the most important players in the clean and simple look that flat design wants to achieve. The usage of a grid in your design is essential to create this white space. Even and balanced elements will create the structure that you would otherwise create using boxes and lines. The following screenshot shows the use of white space on the numbrs.com website:

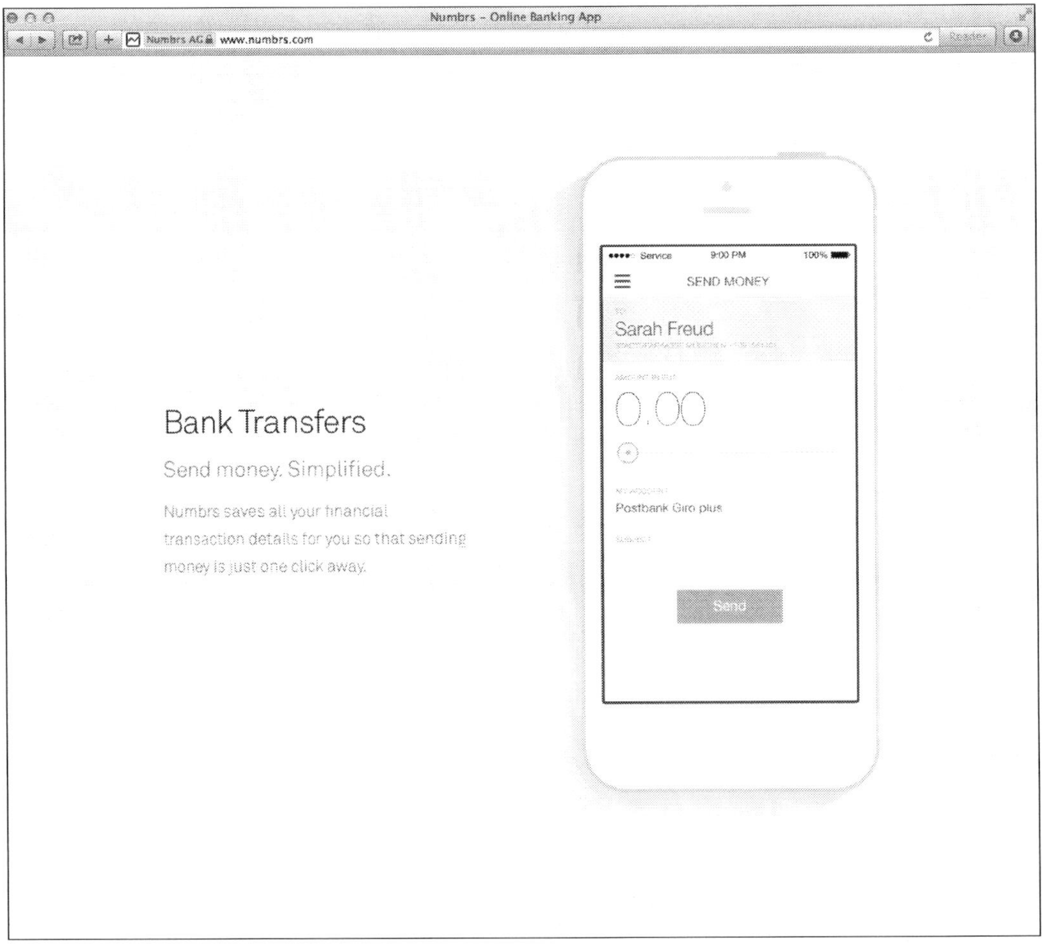

To help you design, there are already several grid systems developed for several kinds of applications. Specifically for the Web, one of the most used ones is the 960 Grid System. It can be found online at `http://960.gs`. The following screenshot shows the 960 Grid System being used on `tapbots.com`:

This grid will allow you to create several types of different blocks based on the most used dimensions, all of which are built with a total width of 960 pixels. You can choose between 12 and 16 columns. These can be used separately or together in the same layout to allow more flexibility on the design of your blocks while maintaining consistency and coherence throughout the project.

If you're looking at creating a responsive website, a good tool to help in this task is unsemantic, which is available online at `http://unsemantic.com/demo-responsive`. This is a grid system that is very similar to 960, but instead of being a fixed grid, this system has a fluid grid. Instead of being defined over a fixed number of columns, the fluid grid is entirely based on percentages, allowing the layout to adapt to the device viewport and provide a responsive experience to the user.

We will learn more about grids and how to use them later on in the book in *Chapter 4, Designing Your Own Flat Website*.

Focusing on typography

Typography is extremely important for a flat design layout. To go along the lines of simplicity and geometric shapes, sans-serif is the definite choice when working with typography in flat. There are a number of typefaces that are more commonly found and used in flat designs. These are chosen as typefaces with their characteristics in mind. These typefaces are usually geometrical; however, with the possibility of having subtle rounded corners, they are are often used in uppercase in titles. This usage of all uppercase letters in a word is also to create a more impactful look for the word, and this can also be achieved by heavier weights on a font. A great font should have a couple of different weights to be able to mix a light weight style with a bold or extrabold one, as this mix of two opposite weights looks good visually, in titles and in text blocks. It gives a greater focus on the title by creating this visual contrast. The following screenshot is an example of the Motiva Sans typeface having different weights. This typeface is available at `http://www.myfonts.com/fonts/niramekko/motiva-sans/`.

Nowadays, plenty of free typefaces with good quality can be found online. These are specially designed for the Web. Websites such as Google Fonts allow users to easily search, browse, and use a typeface on their projects. They are a great tool for web developers who are looking at using custom fonts on their websites.

The following are some of the font families suggested for use in flat design:

- Proxima Nova (`http://www.myfonts.com/fonts/marksimonson/proxima-nova/`)
- Futura (`http://www.myfonts.com/fonts/bitstream/futura/`)
- Lato (`http://www.google.com/fonts/specimen/Lato`)
- Montserrat (`http://www.google.com/fonts/specimen/Montserrat`)
- Open Sans (`http://www.google.com/fonts/specimen/Open+Sans`)
- Cobert (`http://www.fontsquirrel.com/fonts/corbert`)

These are just a couple of typefaces that you may use in your designs. Feel free to search for more that adapt to the style you're aiming at. Depending on what kind of font you get, you can get a more serious tone or a more cheerful one. Choose a font wisely for your project, as the font is one of the main things that is responsible for the look that you create in a website. Ideally, you should choose a maximum of two or three typefaces per website. The main one should be for the titles. This is the most detailed typeface and the one that will set a tone on typography. You should choose another one for the text blocks, which will be your body; this one should be neutral, and its only objective is to make the text readable and make it look in contrast with the titles. The possible third one should be a typeface that works well in uppercase and small sizes; this can be be used in captions, to describe images, or it can be attached to graphics. Choose your typefaces with care; compare and test them to make sure that they go well together. Always keep the medium you're using in mind, as a typeface designed for the screen won't probably work on print, and vice-versa.

Flat colors

The rules for using colors in flat are pretty simple: avoid gradients and textures. These colors should be used as they are, without any modifications. Even a flat color will look like it has a bit of a gradient to it because of the way the LCD screens are built. This is because the color won't be exactly the same in every area of the screen, and also, the light that surrounds your device has some influence on it. So, try to test your colors and choose a palette that works and looks good.

There are some types of preferred colors to be used in flat though. The website, `http://flatuicolors.com`, is great to check these quickly as well as use them. By just clicking on the color on the screen, the hexadecimal code will be copied to your clipboard and be ready to be pasted in your Photoshop or CSS code. The colors shown on the website easily represent the kind of colors used. It's an interesting take on using vivid colors, but they should be toned down a bit. A strong and greener turquoise, a toned-down green, and a slightly less-vivid blue are some of the most used colors. The idea is to create a good color background but one that is not too vivid in order to avoid too much focus on the color. Remember that the color is for the background where the content will be, and the focus should always be on the content and not on the color itself. The following screenshot shows Flat UI Colors from `http://flatuicolors.com`:

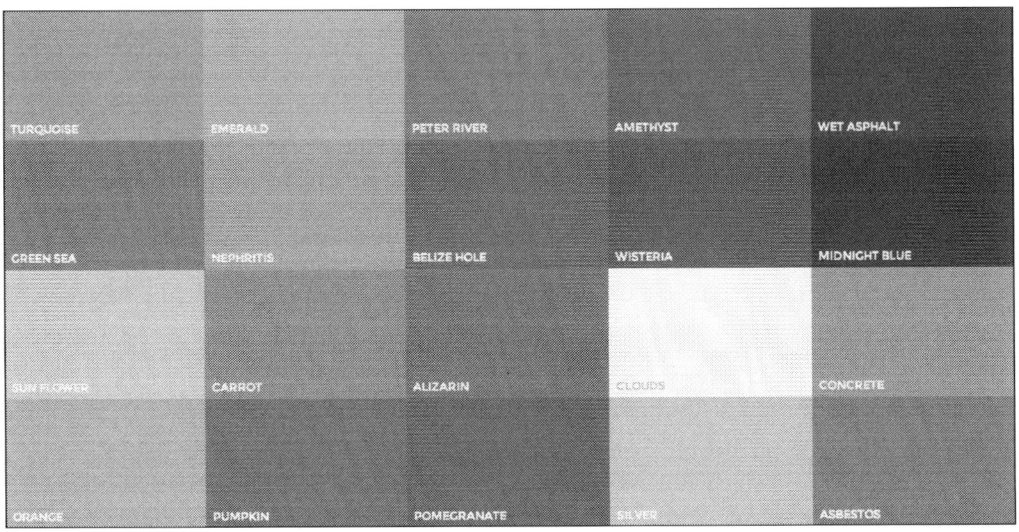

When creating your website, you should choose which color palette you're going to use. This palette is made up of all the colors used in the website and should have one or two main colors and some extra neutral colors. For instance, in the case of patterntap.com (shown in the following screenshot), the main color is obviously that greenish yellow used in the header section, while black is used for the secondary menu at the top, and a very light gray is used for the background. Each color has its own function. Yellow is the main color associated with the brand, and black is a separator. There is a separate content neutral zone, and gray is the content area, where readability is more important. Define your own palette; try to use different shades of the main color, a lighter and a darker one; and test how it works in links, headings, and visual elements such as lines. An important thing to remember while creating a color palette is that you must avoid mixing colors that don't go well together. Also, remember to be coherent in using them. If a heading is light blue in one page, it should be like that in all pages.

> Let me tell you a little secret; when using black for lines or text, try to use a very dark gray instead of complete black. It will look a lot better. Try the same with white; instead of pure white, try to use a grayish or yellowish white. Tinting that color a bit gives the element, where it's applied, another look, just as if you were using a texture.

The following screenshot is an example of the use of flat colors (`www.patterntap.com`):

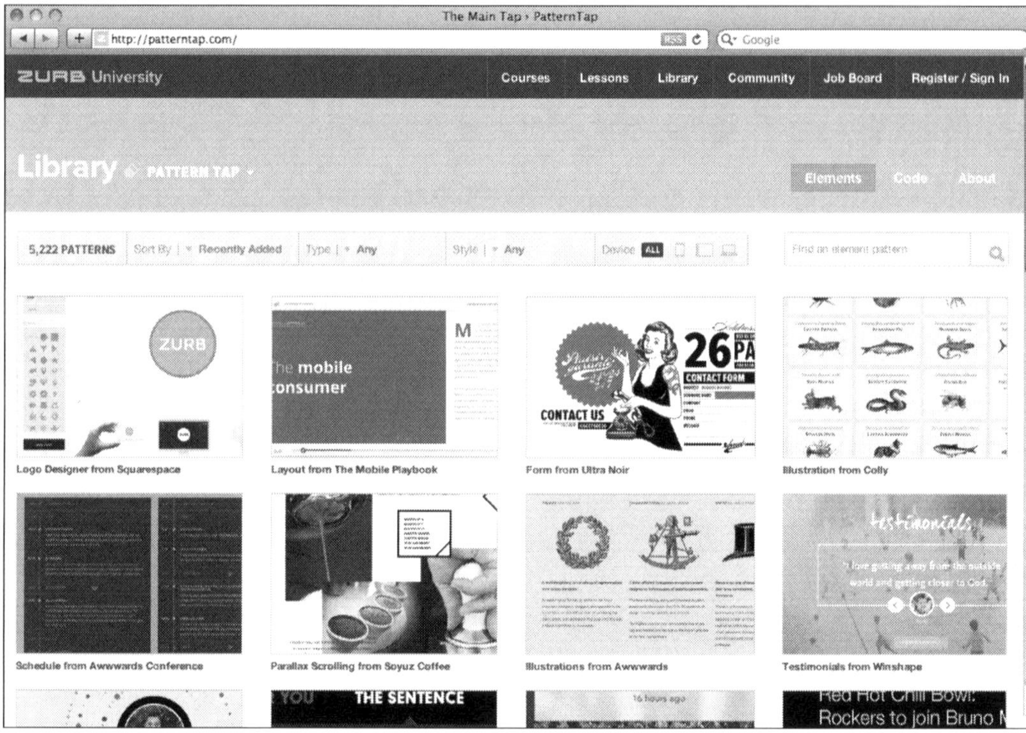

Inspiration and references

There is a lot of know-how needed to work in design, but one of the most important things is visual culture. Feed yourself and your visual culture by looking at other people's work. When learning, try to replicate other people's style and understand how they do what they do, and the most important thing is why they do it like that.

By keeping yourself up to date visually on different projects, you'll find out that you'll visually learn some of the design patterns used, as well as color palettes, interface ideas, layouts, and typography. This is done by just looking at what other people are working on and getting a feel of it visually. You can find some inspiration and good references on flat design and layout later in this section. These are some good examples of execution of flat design that also showcase how to use the style in different ways. Pay attention to the white space, colors, and palettes used, as well as iconography, photography, and how these sites are organized overall. Feel free to use these as an inspiration for your own project by taking ideas on executions and layout, but not by copying an entire layout itself.

A designer's work needs to be original, regardless of the inspirations and/or design patterns used.

The following are some websites that you should know and see for inspiration. These are examples of great execution of the flat design:

- Treehouse (`www.teamtreehouse.com`)

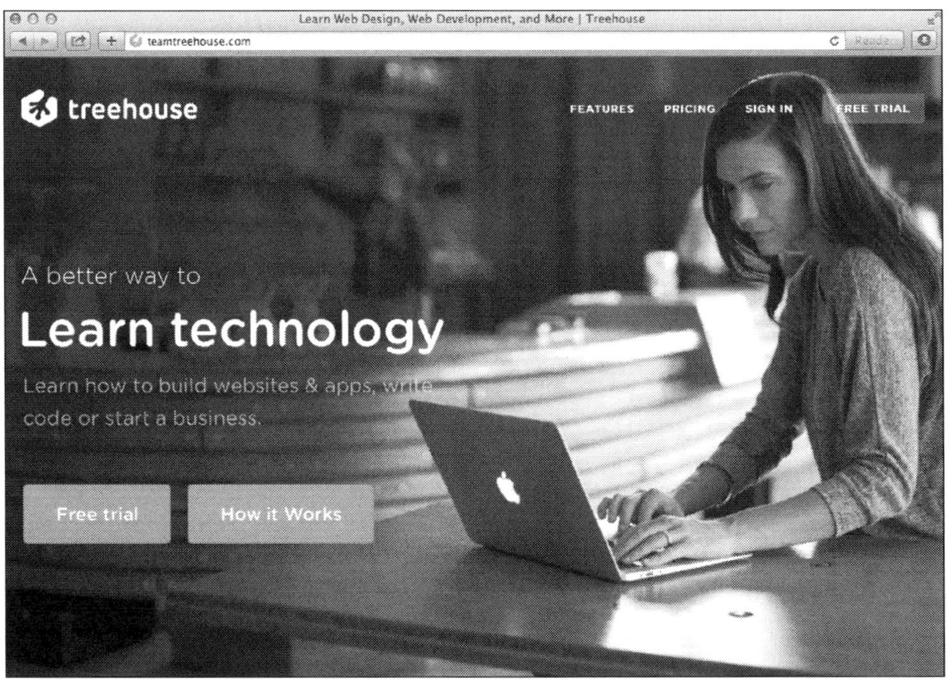

- The Treehouse content section, with flat style illustrations (`www.threehouse.com`)

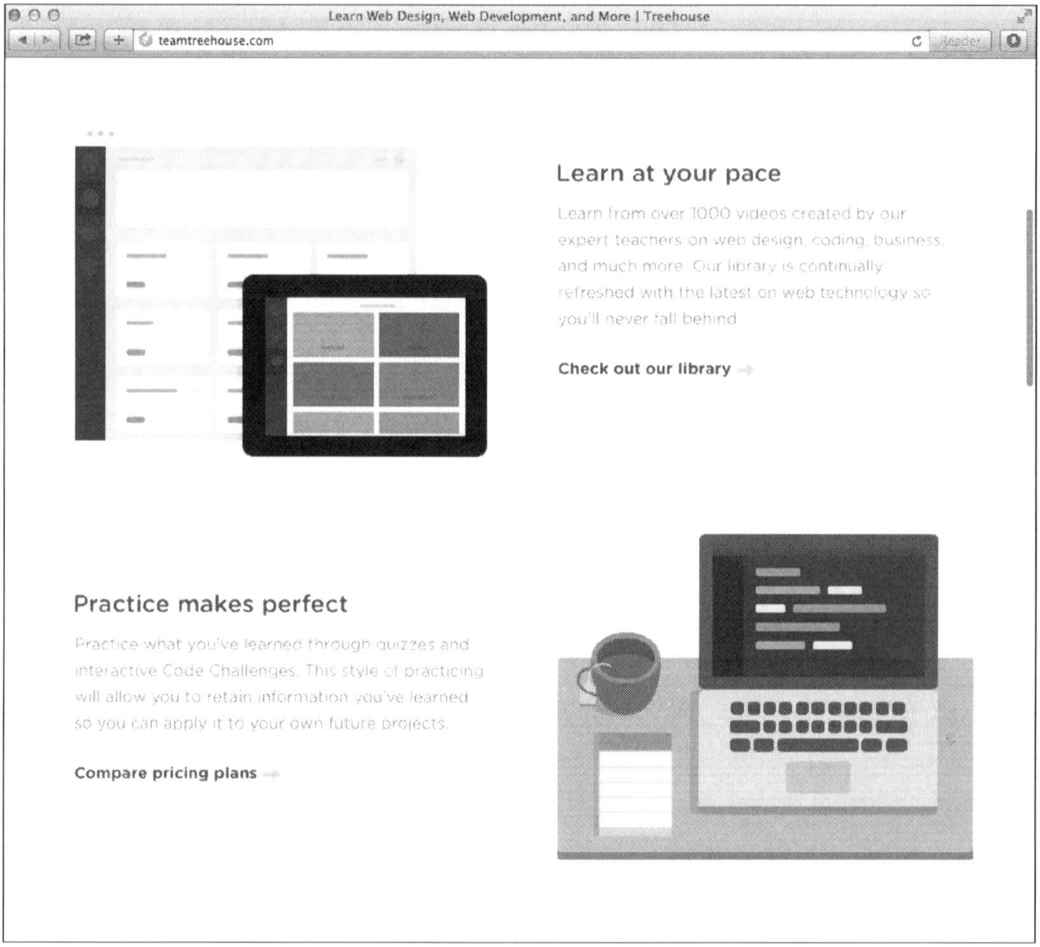

- The Numbrs homepage with full-screen photo using the sans-serif text (`www.numbrs.com`)

- Wacom home page with content blocks and flat icons (`www.wacom.com`)

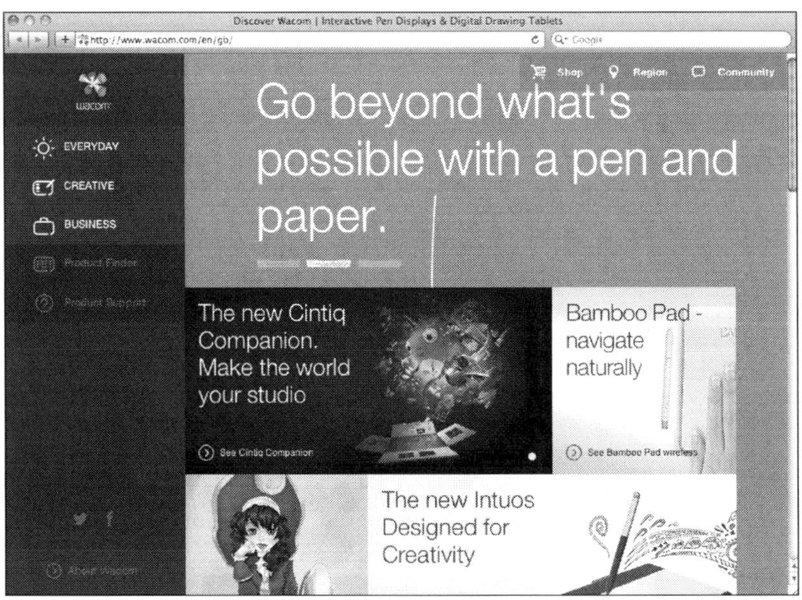

- Hellomonday home page (`www.hellomonday.com`)

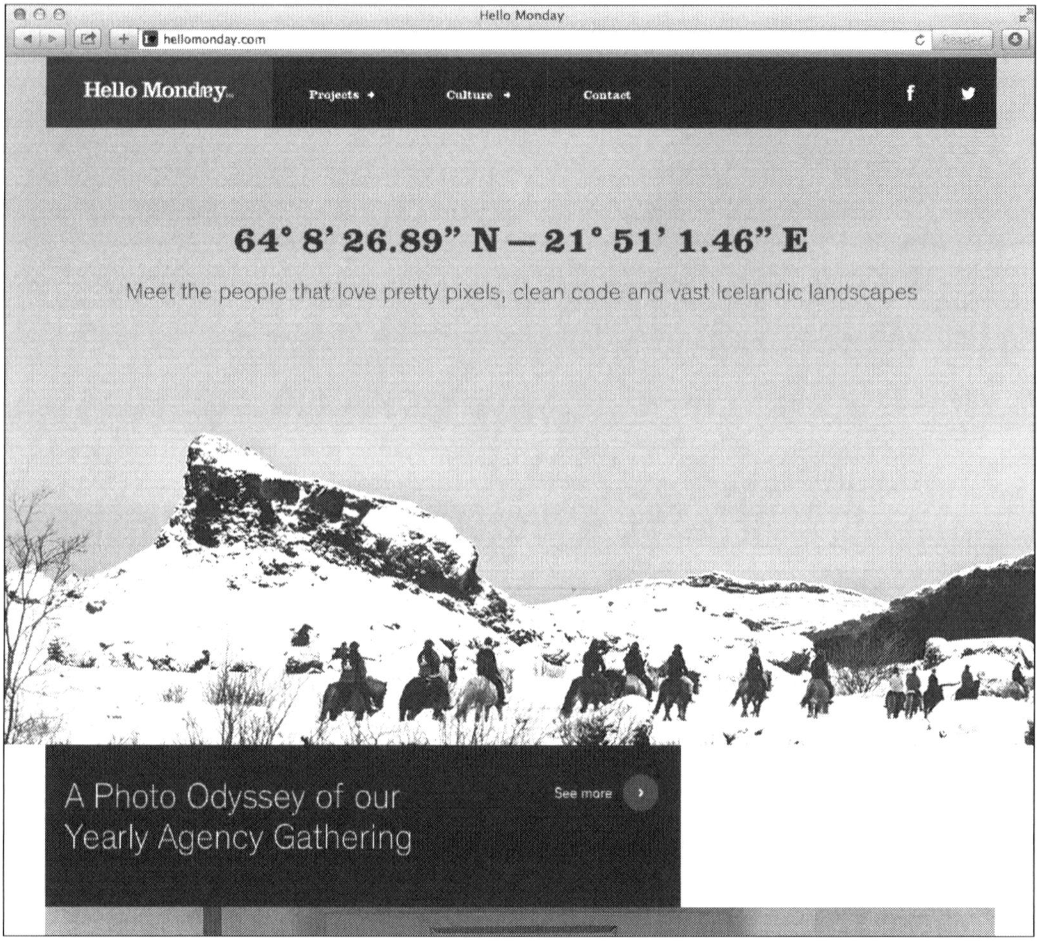

Summary

By now, you should be able to understand the importance of grid and white space on flat design as well as how to create impactful messaging using great typography over flat colors. Flat design is all about the detail, and in this case, the detail is in learning how to design with the lack of complexity and noise. Now you know how to make it look good. In the next chapter, we will learn how to make it work well by going over web usability and its importance in flat interfaces.

3
Creating a Flat and Usable Interface

This chapter will cover web usability on flat design and how important this is for the functioning of every website and web application's design in flat design, since this style may create several usability problems given its simple look. We will cover this by understanding what web usability is and by learning to design a web form with usability in mind, learning which elements and what the designer needs to pay attention to, to successfully create a usable interface.

Understanding web usability

Jakob Nielsen, a web usability consultant and usability expert, defines usability in the website, `http://www.nngroup.com/articles/usability-101-introduction-to-usability/`, as follows:

> "*Usability is a quality attribute that assesses how easy user interfaces are to use. The word usability also refers to methods for improving ease-of-use during the design process.*"

In this case, web usability relates to the good functioning of a website and how easy and predictable it is for the user. We, as designers and developers, assume that for most people using a website is easy and a skill that is already considered natural, but this is not an assumption that you should make. On the contrary, when designing a website or an interface, you must assume that the user doesn't have prior experience in using them. An interface must be designed in such a way that it is intuitive and easy to use, even for a first-time user.

All elements must be visually identifiable. Elements such as links, forms, text fields, and buttons must be easily distinguishable. For instance, a link is historically and usually represented—as it was defined on the first version of HTML—by a blue underlined word in a block of text, but this is not always the case, mainly due to customization and color scheming created by web designers. This means that even without using this standard notation of a hyperlink, there should be a simple way for the user to identify this element in a block of text. It has to be natural, and the user must understand this by himself or herself, without the need for any explanation. Usually, this is done by keeping the underline in the word and changing the color to a color that contrasts with the text color. The underline can be replaced by bold text effect to clarify that this specific word is different from the regular reading text.

The rollover effect is also very important. When hovering the mouse cursor over the word, the user detects a difference in the word; sometimes, the underline disappears or there's a bold effect applied to the word. However, regardless of the effect or style chosen, there's a visual change in the link. This change is what's responsible for giving the user the feeling that this specific element, which responds to interaction, is considered an important element that will have more functions than just simple text, as is the case with a hyperlink, which will take the user to a different page.

This is the kind of thought that the user goes through when visiting a web page, and this is one example of how usability works in web design. Usability is even more important when talking about a web or mobile app, since in this case, there is a specific user journey that must exist to allow the user to accomplish certain tasks. This is because the app is a tool with a specific objective. However, in a website, the content is to be accessed depending on the interest of the visitors and their own objectives.

Unfortunately, the importance of usability is often disregarded, but it should always be a part of your work in every web design project. It is especially important in flat given its look, but why is usability important?

The importance of web usability

Usability is important for several reasons. The first and foremost reason being, usability guarantees that your website *just works*.

When creating any given project, there's always an objective. Usually the objective is to inform the visitor by showing images and text content, but it can also be to sell a product or service or even provide a service directly in the case of a web application. Regardless of what kind of objective it is, there is always one. Usability is the tool for you and the designer to make sure that everything works so that you achieve that objective. By making sure that the user understands the website navigation or by clarifying an action by pressing a button, you're making it easier and more probable that a user will follow the expected user journey.

If you're running a commercial website, this is especially important, because it will have a direct impact on your revenue and can be the difference between a successful or failed online business. In one case, a website made an additional 300 million dollars in a year just by changing a simple button (`http://www.uie.com/articles/three_hund_million_button/`). This definitely makes a big case for usability.

Having usability in mind when designing a website is often the difference between keeping and losing a visitor. If the user doesn't understand the website or if they can't easily find what they're looking for, frustration kicks in, and the user will leave, to look for that piece of content elsewhere. You probably know this feeling, when you are looking for something that is incredibly hard to find in a confusing website. Try to imagine what your users will think when using a website and make sure that you avoid all the frustrations that might arise.

If you feel that you already had the basic usability problems and still believe that you could improve your work, you probably need to start testing. One of the the best tools to understand what is failing in your website is user testing, that is, sitting down with a user and going through the website with him or her and learning from his or her feedback.

There are a lot of different ways to test a website, and if you're interested in learning more about web usability, I definitely recommend Jakob Nielsen's book, *Designing Web Usability*, available on Amazon at `http://www.amazon.co.uk/Designing-Web-Usability-Practice-Simplicity/dp/156205810X`.

Achieving a good balance

OK, so now that we covered what web usability is and you know how badly it can affect a website's visitor, I want you to take a step back, relax, and not panic. You're probably already avoiding most of the larger usability issues just by using common sense as any designer making decisions for a specific design should do. We don't want to make a website so clear and foolproof that it lacks style and color. After all, innovation comes from being bold and trying different things.

This being said, your ultimate objective is to achieve a good balance between a really great-looking website and a functional one. Most of the times, usability is just about organization and common sense, and this is a way of working rather than a technique to be applied. A more innovative interface will be harder to use in the beginning, but the designer can choose to take this risk to achieve a different experience. However, if you're looking at playing safe, try to focus on known and familiar types of layouts and simple designs.

Sometimes, usability improvements are achieved by making really small and simple adjustments to a website's design.

There are several designers proposing redesigns of well-known websites, and most of them focus on simplifying the current layouts by reorganizing, simplifying, or even redesigning elements. Reorganization and simplification of elements is a great exercise, because it makes you understand which elements are really important on a design and which are merely decorative.

The Swedish agency Weare1910 (`http://weare1910.com/`) created a redesign proposal for Wikipedia (`http://en.wikipedia.org`), where they redesign the website to focus more on the content while simplifying the design at the same time. This was done by vastly improving typography by making the text as well as the line height larger and improving the readability of the articles, while at the same time, simplifying the layout by removing the menu on the left-hand side. This created a simpler but identifiable version of the Wikipedia website. The following screenshot (`http://blog.weare1910.com/post/75576312730/a-readable-wikipedia`) shows Wikipedia (at the top) and its redesign (at the bottom).

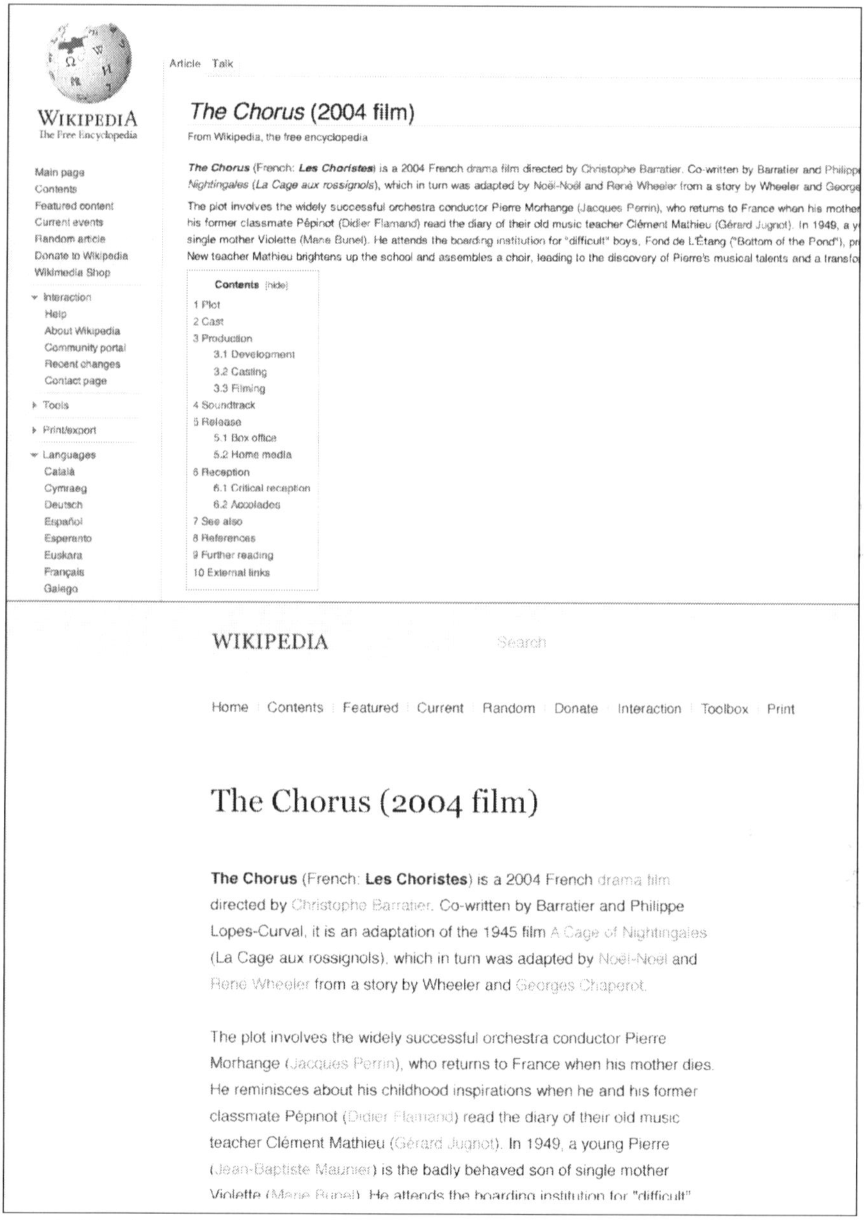

Wikipedia (top) and redesign (bottom). Available at http://blog.weare1910.com

So, to have a clear look at this, let's do a small exercise of simplifying a design. I chose the homepage of the *Transport for London* website, since it's an older website, and its design is still very clunky and looks really cluttered. This is in no way a serious redesign but just a way of learning how some simplification on a design creates a lighter and more readable page.

First, let's get the original website on which we can work. You can open the `tfl-redesign.psd` file provided with this book and work on it.

> **Downloading the example code**
>
> You can download the example code files for all Packt books you have purchased from your account at `http://www.packtpub.com`. If you purchased this book elsewhere, you can visit `http://www.packtpub.com/support` and register to have the files e-mailed directly to you.

With the file open, let's identify which blocks to work on. Focus just on the content section and ignore the bar on the right-hand side. We will divide the website into three main sections: the main highlights section, the middle section with oyster charges and Barclays information, and the last section with other news and important information. These are the sections we will redesign. The following screenshot shows the old TFL website (`www.tfl.gov.uk`) on the left-hand side and the main content sections that are identified on the right-hand side:

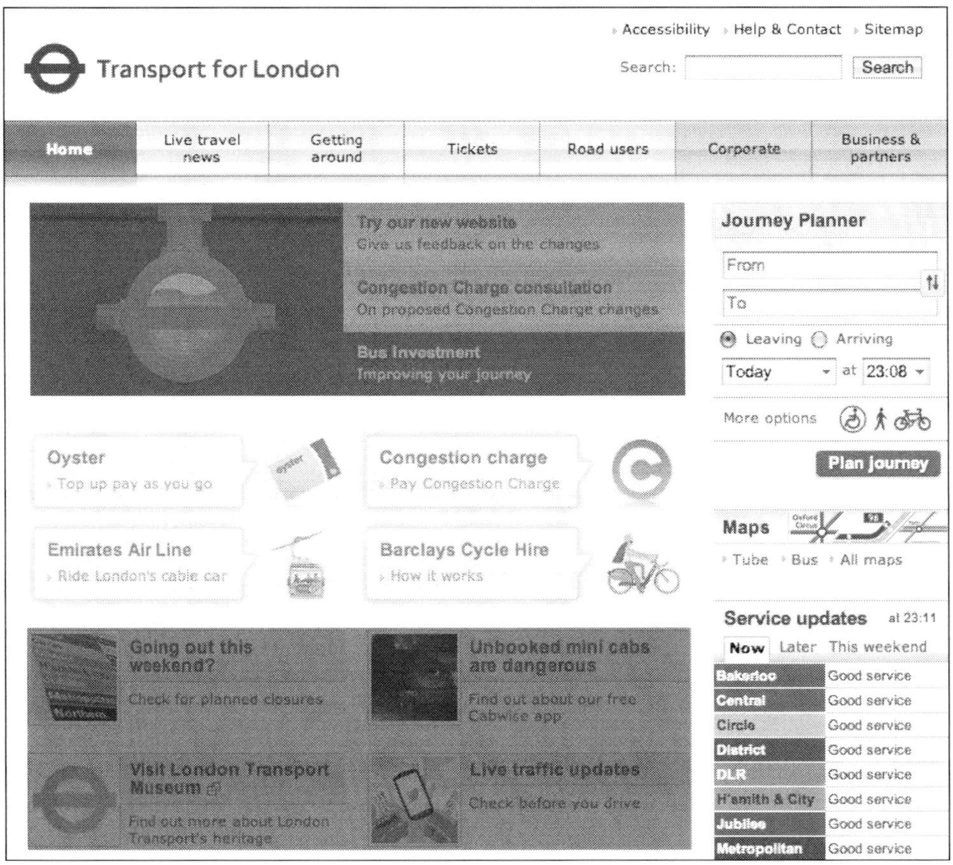

TFL website www.tfl.gov.uk (left) and main content sections identified (right)

With our sections identified and highlighted, let's start replacing this with our content. For the first section, create similar titles and body texts and overlay the current design so that we can align the content in the same element.

So, rewrite the titles of the first section. You can use the Lato font to do this. Set the size of the text to 13 pt the weight of the titles to black, to set these apart from the description text. The first two blocks are disabled, so let's set the color of the text as gray (`#979797`). This will give the look of a faded black color and will visually hint that these blocks are disabled, in contrast to the enabled and active one. Since we are removing the blue background, we can't keep the text white. So set the active line title as blue; just pick the color of the background and set the bottom line as black.

You now have the content of the first section. Just select the image and delete it and paint that part white to match the background. To improve the division between these section content lines, let's create some dividing lines. Create two lines of 1 px weight in between the texts and set it as gray (`#dcdcdc`). This will help define the blocks visually while still keeping them very simple and light, as is evident in the following screenshot:

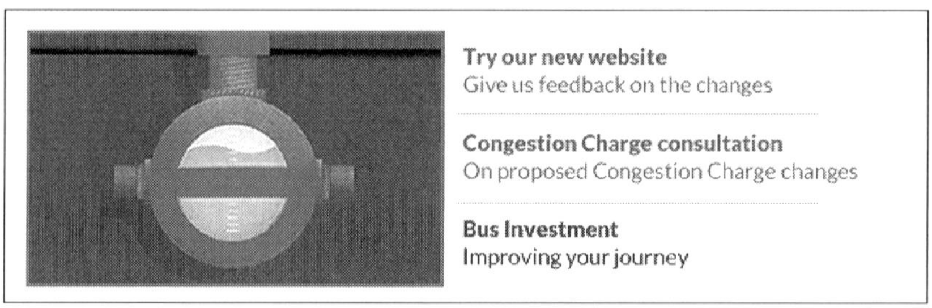

Moving on to the next section, let's do the same and replace the text by overlaying it. Copy the color of the same text and ignore the green triangle. Align the text to the left of the block and delete the image and text that were there before. The following screenshot shows how the page should look after doing all this:

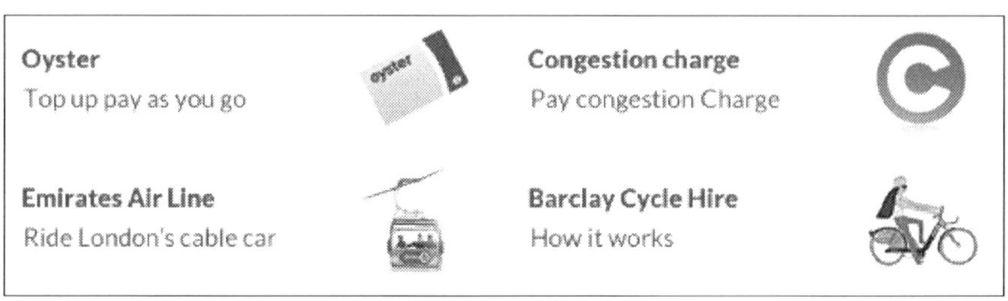

Do the same for the final section, aligning the title with the top of the image and keeping the same colors. The final result will look similar to the following screenshot:

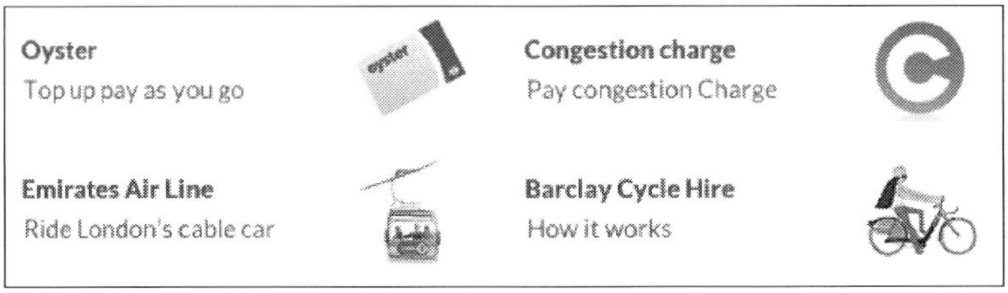

Now that we have all the sections simplified, we can already tell that the page looks lighter and cleaner. However, without the lines and boxes, the content seems less congested. So, we need to give a larger spacing between the blocks, to make them visually separated. Just pull down some pixels of sections two and three, and it will be enough to give the feeling of different sections. The result of the simplified TFL website will look similar to the following screenshot:

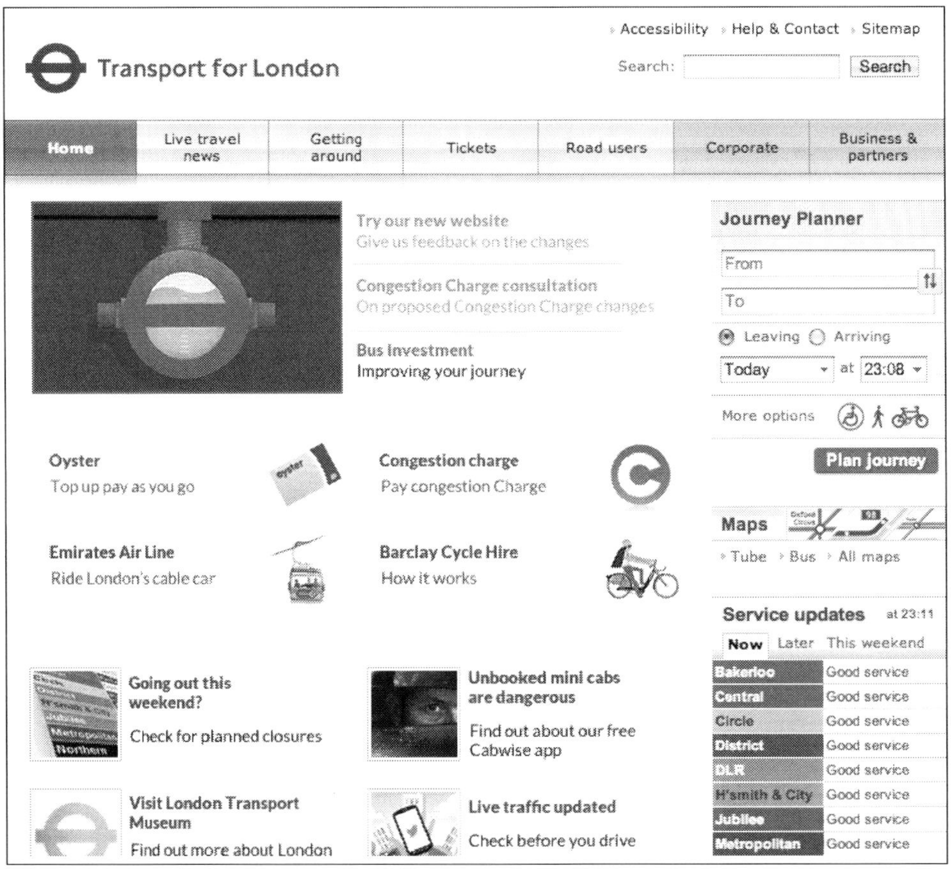

You can see a clear improvement in the result of these simple changes. In fact, the changes were no more that just removing the background images and nonessential images from the layout in a way that the content defines the block instead of boxes and lines. This led to the creation of more whitespace and made the website lighter. This is evident in the following screenshot:

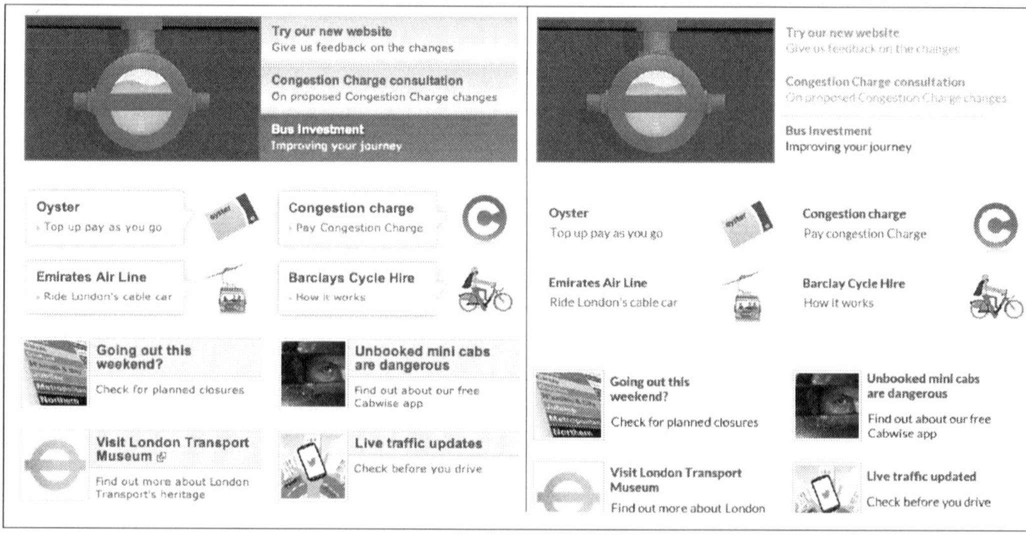

Web forms usability

As we said earlier, usability is extremely important in a flat design. The element that suffers more on the usability front from this style is usually the **web form**. It is usually so easy to match controls such as buttons and text fields to match the flat styles that they lose the effects and features that make them identifiable. A text field is usually represented by a rectangular box with a subtle inner shadow to show that it is expecting content. This shadow is often lost in flat design, and to avoid this, we need to make sure that a form is identifiable as a form. There are several ways of doing this. The best way to do this is by laying your hands on it, so let's do a simple exercise on web forms usability.

Next, we will create a simple sign-up form for a website. To do this, we will use the `ele_winvista_firefox_all.psd` file, which is available on the resource pack that accompanies this book. It is also available online at `http://designerstoolbox.com/designresources/elements/vista/firefox/`.

This file is a browser form template, with the elements that you'd find when creating a basic HTML form rendered in Firefox. So, let's begin.

Creating a web form with regular browser styles

Let's execute the following steps to create a web form:

1. Create a new file of size 350 x 350 px in Photoshop. We will create our form in this file.
2. Create a text field with the text `Name`. This field will serve as the title template for the remaining fields. You can define the font as Arial and set the size to 14 pt.
3. Now that you have the title, copy the **Input Field** folder from your template file into your new document. Align them side by side with the title on the left-hand side and the text field on the right-hand side, as shown in the following screenshot:

4. We need to organize our file and save the title and field in a folder with the name corresponding to the field. Duplicate the `name` folder and let's change it to `Age`.
5. Now, let's create a `Gender` field. To do this, we are going to use the template for the pull-down list and assign it with a title of its own.
6. Let's assume that we're creating a form for a blog, so we will need an account type selector. We'll then create a field named `Account`, with radio buttons. Copy the `Selected Radio Button` and `Unselected Radio Button` folders and change the text to `Author` and `Reviewer`, respectively. These are the two different account statuses that the blog will have, with different permissions.
7. To finish, copy the `Button` folder into your file and align it to the right.
8. Our standard form is completed! This is how a simple HTML form would look in a Firefox browser, and this is one of the standard looks. You should end up with a design like the following screenshot:

That's it, pretty simple right? However, it's a pretty standard, "not exciting" look. So, next let's try it out with some flat design style.

Recreating the form with flat style

Now that we have our basic form, we need to recreate the elements to match the flat design look. To do this, let's use the font we used earlier, Lato, and recreate the form using the following steps:

1. Duplicate the file we created and name it `flat-form.psd`. We will use the file that we created earlier as our foundation to create this new form.
2. Change the font of the title to Lato and set its size to 15 pt.
3. For the text field, create a 190 px wide and 35 px high white rectangle. This will be our new flat text field.
4. Add a blending option such as stroke to this rectangle. The stroke should be of size 1 px and positioned inside the rectangle. We don't want the border to be very strong; we want it to be subtle and lighter than the text. So, let's define its color as `#aeaeae`. This light gray will work great on top of white and with black text.

5. Now, let's just create our filler text like we had earlier and change its size to 13 pt; we just made our first flat form element. It should look like the following screenshot:

6. Duplicate the new field to use it for `Age` and `Gender`. On `Gender`, we can use the same rectangle, but we're going to add a small triangle to indicate that it's a pull-down list. To create this triangle, we will use the Polygon Tool (U) and create a shape with three sides. Set the triangle as black or the same gray of the border (`#aeaeae`), and the pull-down button is created.
7. This is a personal option and it depends on your taste. To create a greater focus on the button, we can use the inverted option of the button, make the triangle white, and create a rectangle with the same color as the rectangle border. To do this, duplicate the rectangle we're using for the text field, and change its width to 35 px. Delete the layer style that is defining the stroke, as we don't need it here, and define the color of this rectangle as `#aeaeae`. This will create a contrast on the field and further differentiate it from the other fields being used.
8. For the account form, we'll recreate the circular element with the Ellipse Tool. Create a 16 x 16 px white circle with the same stroke. Align it with the other fields. This will be our radio button. Duplicate this layer and shrink it to 9 x 9 px; delete the stroke and define the main color as `#aeaeae`. This will be our selection. For the option text, let's use the same text field and just shift it to the right, so we can have the radio button on the left-hand side. Now, we just duplicate this line, pull it down, delete the selected layer, and we have the unselected radio button. It should look like the following screenshot:

9. Now, we're only missing the button. For that, we'll use the same rectangle we're using for the field, remove the stroke, set the background to `#aeaeae`, and change its width to 105 px. We can use the `title` text field with the text color set to white to create the label.

So now, we have exactly the same form as the one we had earlier, but it is redesigned in a flat design style. As you can see, this is made up of very simple and basic elements and looks more minimalistic than the original version. We're only using black, gray, and white. However, you can choose to use the main brand color on the rectangle stroke and backgrounds when working on a website that features more colors, to bring it more in line with the design created. The following screenshot shows the default style form (on the left-hand side) and the flat style form (on the right-hand side):

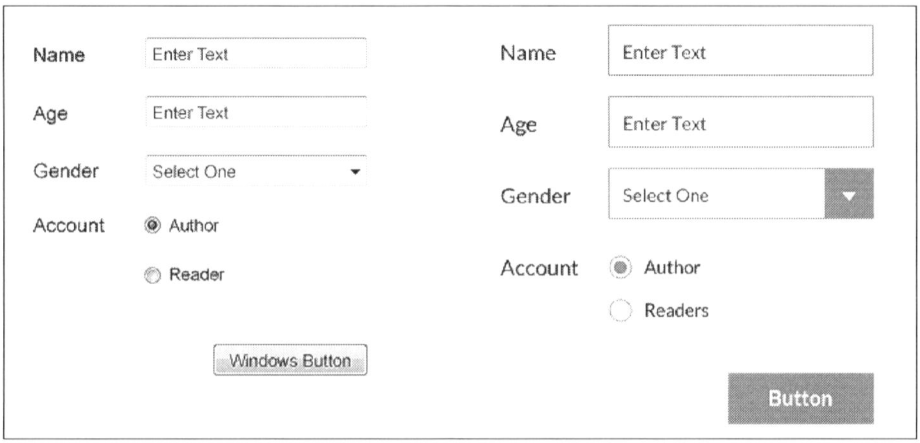

Refining the form's usability

As you can notice, our new form resembles the default version in terms of the positioning and the way the elements work, but we can still improve its usability to make sure that the user has the best experience possible. Now, let's do a few of the following small adjustments that will greatly improve the form:

1. First, let's change the text inside the fields. Currently, this text is set to black and reads **Enter Text**. This text is known as the placeholder text and should be used to indicate to the user the kind of content that the website is expecting. You can use actions or content example here to show the user which content he or she should input. Let's change the text to `Enter your name`, as this will help the user in filling this field. However, black is a color that we reserve for the content, so in order to make this look more discrete and less like content, we'll set the text to gray (`#aeaeae`). This way, the user has a visual hint, but without black text, the field still looks empty and ready for the user to fill it.
2. Do the same for the **Age** field, but use the `Enter your age` text.

3. Change the text in **Gender** to `Select your gender`, thus making the reference to the selection box.
4. Finally, change the text of the button to the action of the form. In this case, since this is a registration form, change the text to register. This small change will define the main action of the form to the user, making sure that the user understands what action he or she is performing on the website. Colors can also be used in buttons to indicate certain actions. For example, a **Delete Account** button will provide the benefit of having a red background, to indicate a permanent and extreme action, such as the deletion of an account.

These changes are extremely simple but pretty effective in optimizing and improving the usability of this form. These are some of the bits you should focus on while designing forms to ensure performance and ease of use. Your screen should look similar to what is shown in the following screenshot:

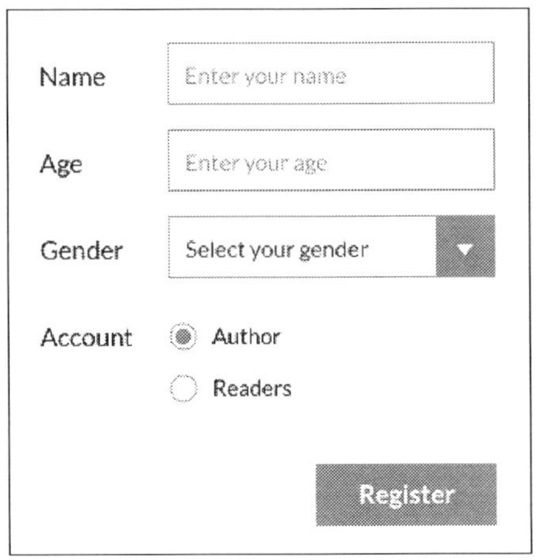

Flat readability

Flat design usually features large sans-serif typefaces used for messaging and titles. These bits of text look great over photos and flat colors, but as with everyone, you always have to make sure that your typography is readable. In the case of flat, where you're not supposed to use drop shadows or gradients, you have to be extra careful about readability. For this, always look to achieve the best contrast between text and background.

Let's do a quick exercise using the following steps to try out the best ways to achieve good readability:

1. Create a new document on Photoshop, where we will try the colors. We just want to overlay text on top of blocks, so create a small rectangle of size 160 x 175 px. Set the color of this shape as black, and create a text field inside of it in white. This contrast, white on top of black, is extremely readable. The best contrast for readability is, of course, black on top of white, like every book and every newspaper. We just created the inverse of this contrast, which is also extremely easy to read and works well with titles. I wouldn't recommend that you should read white text on top of black as it's extremely tiring for the eyes.
2. Let's now try with one of the flat colors from `http://flatuicolors.com/`, which we talked about earlier, and define the color of the shape as `#4d9ad7`. This color looks really great, as it's subtle and vibrant at the same time, and the white text reads extremely well, as white contrasts well with this vivid shade of blue.
3. Repeat the previous steps with the `#65c378`, `#9166b2`, and `#374a5d` colors. All these will read great in white as they are vivid and darker colors.
4. Now change one of the words in the text to black. You will notice that even though the text is still readable, the contrast doesn't feel quite right. Black is a color that is only very readable on top of very light colors, and in this case, it just loses a bit of the sharpness that white offers us. We're not able to see it clearly in the following screenshot, but you can test this yourself by following this exercise and checking the examples that are given with this book:

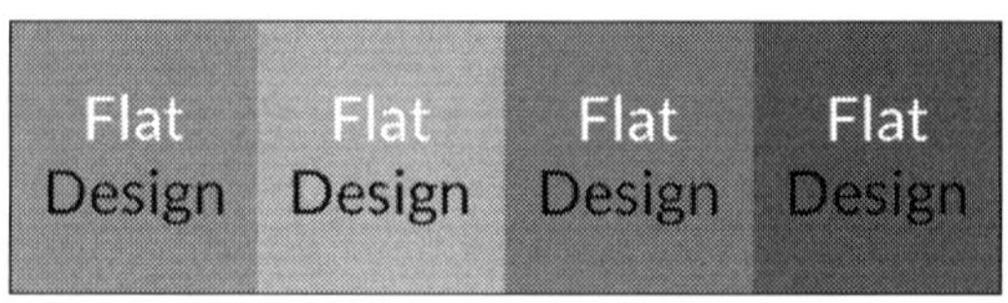

5. Let's now try some different weights. In a color tile, write `Flat Design Rules` in three lines. Change the weight of `Flat` to light, `Design` to regular, and `Rules` to black. This way, we can see how the typeface looks in different weights. Light looks really great and creates a more minimalistic and light look, while black creates a bigger contrast by creating a bigger and visually larger text block. This is good for titles and to create a more impactful messaging option. Be especially careful with light typefaces, as they can sometimes lack readability by being too thin. However, as always, we should test the light typeface, as we are doing right now.

6. With colored text, it's easier to have contrast problems. Try text with green (`#65c378`) on top of a blue block (`#4d9ad7`) and the inverse of it. This combination has poor readability, and you should avoid it. There are some complementary colors that you can use. These are colors that are opposite to one another in the color wheel and have a greater contrast. If you're looking at using colored text on top of a colored background, make sure they have a good contrast to ensure readability. Your screen should now look similar to what is shown in the following screenshot:

7. When using an image background, you have to be especially careful with the placement of your text, as images have different shapes and colors. Ideally, you'll want to position your text on top of the image with a flat color.

These are the main problems relating to the readability of text on flat design that you can encounter, and these are some good tests that you can perform with your website color palette and typeface. Remember that each type has specific heights and shapes, and you have to be careful when choosing which weight to use. Try them out and look for inspiration; you'll know you found your perfect font when you see it applied on your website.

Summary

In this chapter, we covered the basic definition of web usability and how important it is, especially in flat design, to make sure that you create great and functional interfaces. We saw how usability can be achieved with small changes, remembering that the focus should be on making the interface as easy as possible for the user. We also covered web usability in web forms, one of the elements that usually has more usability problems in flat, and how to avoid them as well as convert the form to the flat style. We also went through flat types and learned how to test readability in several cases.

4

Designing Your Own Flat Website

This chapter will be a practical step-by-step guide on how to design a simple website in flat design style.

In this chapter, we will cover the following topics:

- Project planning
- Using external resources to simplify and speed up the work
- The layout design process
- Creating a design by keeping its development in mind to speed up the whole work process

Planning your work

Planning is definitely one of the most important stages in designing a website. Most of the work boils down to knowing exactly what and how you will design and develop your website; planning is where all these decisions will be made.

You need to first define your target and your website objective, what you want to achieve, and for whom. Imagine that you're creating an online e-commerce website for a gadget company. The objective will be to sell those gadgets online (the "what"), and the target would be men of the age group of 25 to 50 (the "who"). These are usually pretty simple to understand. However, in case you ever find yourself with an unclear briefing from a client, make sure that you understand their objectives and targets beforehand, because there's nothing worse than an uninformed designer working on a project.

However, in this case, we're creating our own portfolio page. So, essentially, we're creating a page intended to showcase our work (the "what") to designers and possible future clients (the "who"). Of course, the target in this case is not as easily defined as a toy company or a women's clothing store, but the target always exists. You can be a designer who is more interested in mobiles or fashion, so try to have this in mind when designing your website. Your online and offline images should make the viewer associate you to a certain market, and this is done by creating and implementing a specific approach and style to your home page design.

Unfortunately, I won't get to know you personally, so we'll have to create a simple and flexible designer portfolio. This should be something that can be used for a general portfolio, regardless of your work specialty. So, let's get down to planning!

Defining your sections

Since we're designing a portfolio, the focus is on showing the work of the designer. We will have just a couple of sections here; they are as follows:

- **Work/Portfolio**: This is a place to showcase your design projects
- **About**: This is a small text description of you as a designer and person, and your experience
- **Contact**: This is a place to store your contacts so that the viewer can contact you, and your location

These are the essential sections we will have to design for your portfolio. Since this is such a small and simple site, we'll create a one-page website. This kind of page is being used more and more lately. This is mainly because it presents the user with all the information really quickly and in a very simple way. Also, it provides a more dynamic experience by presenting different content on just a single page.

Start designing your page

So now that we know what we're going to design, we are ready to start sketching and designing your website. I usually start by creating a really simple sketch on paper just to mock really quickly what we're going to design. You can also use software such as Balsamiq to create your wireframes, but I prefer to start sketching on paper. So, grab a piece of paper and start sketching.

The page we're going to create will feature five visual blocks. These blocks are as follows:

- **Header**: This is where we will put an avatar or logo to represent the designer as a brand and the menu
- **About**: This is the about section with a text about you and a link to your resume
- **Projects**: This is the section to feature your design work with thumbnails
- **Contacts**: This is a short text block with your contacts
- **Footer**: This is a really small block by the end of the page with copyright and links for social networks

  The following diagram is my rough sketch:

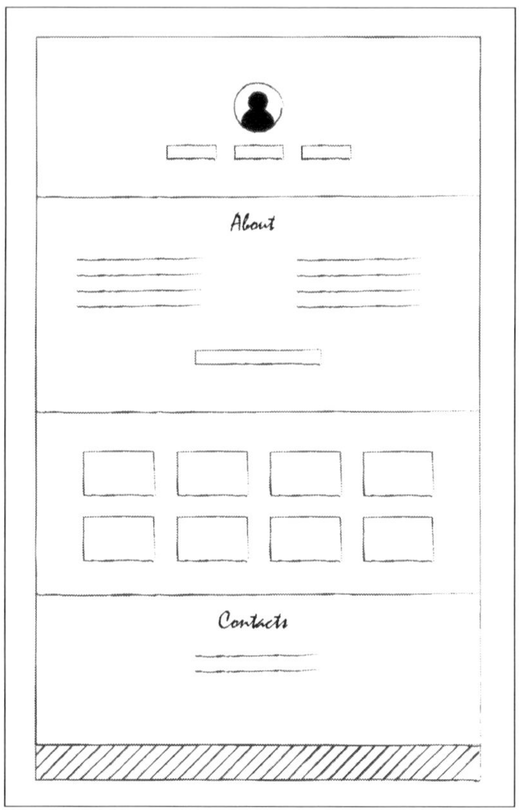

A hand-drawn layout

With our layout drawn out, we're ready to open Photoshop and start designing our final page.

Using the Designmodo.com Flat UI

With so many designers and developers out there, you can find several external resources and predesigned and predeveloped components that you can use to save time on your projects. The Designmodo.com Flat UI pack is a great pack to use in your projects, with some of the essential elements already designed, so we'll use it to design our page. You can get the free pack, which includes a layered PSD, icons, Lato font, and files for our development with Twitter Bootstrap 3-based framework ready to use at `http://designmodo.com/flat-free/`. Later on in this book, we'll be using these predeveloped components to set up our page for our development work and bring our layout to life. The following is a screenshot of the Designmodo Flat UI pack:

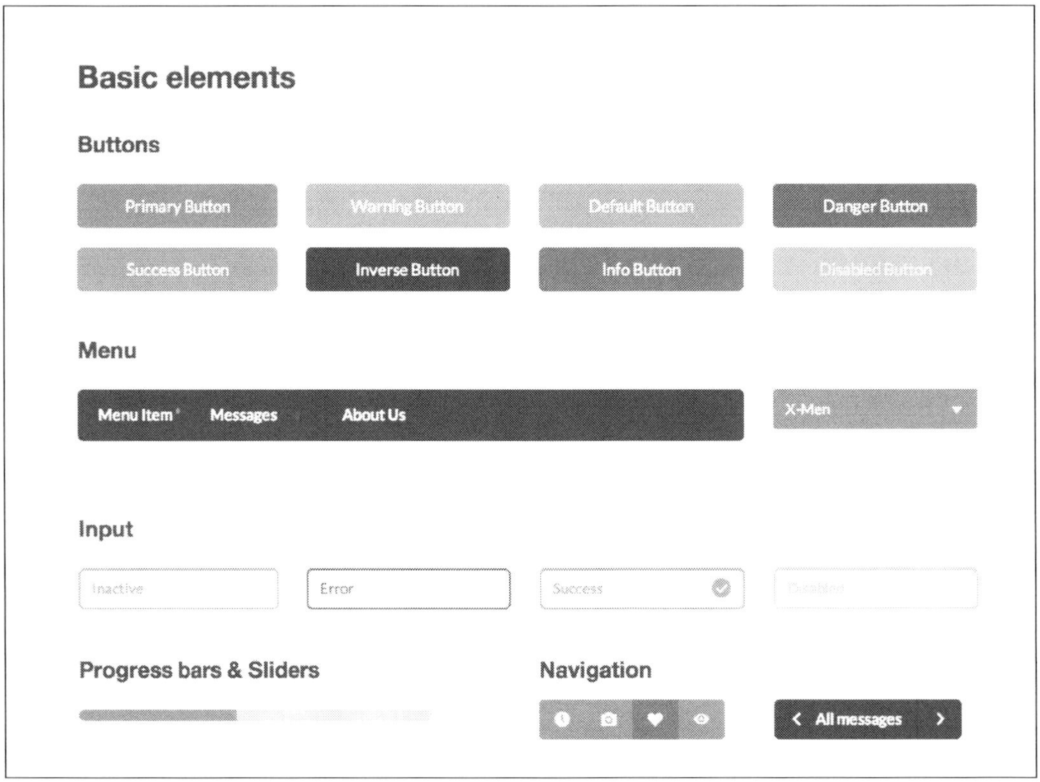

Designing in Photoshop

Now that we have our sections defined and our global layout drawn out, we're ready to start creating our final pixels. So, open your Photoshop, and let's get down to business and execute the following steps:

1. Create a new document that is 1200 px wide and 2000 px high and has a white background. This will be the canvas with our full-length website design.
2. Let's start by creating our header. We'll need to use an avatar for our face, so while you can use your own avatar, I'll grab one from `http://uifaces.com/`, where you can find several avatars of real users to use in your design mockups.
3. Let's create a shape that will serve as our header background with the rectangle tool. You can set the color of the shape to gray, as we will decide on the colors later on.
4. Now that we have the foundation for our header, let's put or avatar/logo in it. This will be our branding area of the website. It shows what the website is about and who it belongs to.
5. Create a 125 x 125 px circle and use it as a mask for your avatar. Give the mask a white stroke blending option with 5 px. This will create a border around our circle to make the avatar pop a bit more.
6. To create our menu, we'll use text fields. Create three different text fields and write `ABOUT`, `WORK`, and `CONTACTS` in them. These will be our menu links. Set the text with the font type as Lato, font style as Bold, and text size as 20 px. This is where you can experiment with the text style; try using lowercase text instead of uppercase and try a lighter weight and underline for these. You can adapt the links to the style of your choice, but I'll stick to the ones indicated, as I believe it works and looks good.
7. So, our header is created. We're only missing the color. Let's go to `http://flatuicolors.com/` and get one of the colors suggested there. As I mentioned earlier in *Chapter 3, Creating a Flat and Usable Interface*, we're setting the main color of our color scheme for the whole website by choosing this color. So, keep this in mind when choosing a color. Usually, I prefer building my color palette throughout the design of the site, as I'm able to try them out instantly. Choose the one of your liking; I'll use Peter River, `#3498db`.

The following screenshot shows how your header should look by now:

8. If you want to create an even more interesting and impactful header, you can also use a background image for the header. If you have an image of your work desk or your computer with the working files visible on your screen, these are great to represent your work. Put it below the colored background layer and change the color layer opacity to around 85 percent. This will create a blue tint effect on the image. The following screenshot shows a blue tint background found at `http://sendtoinc.com/`:

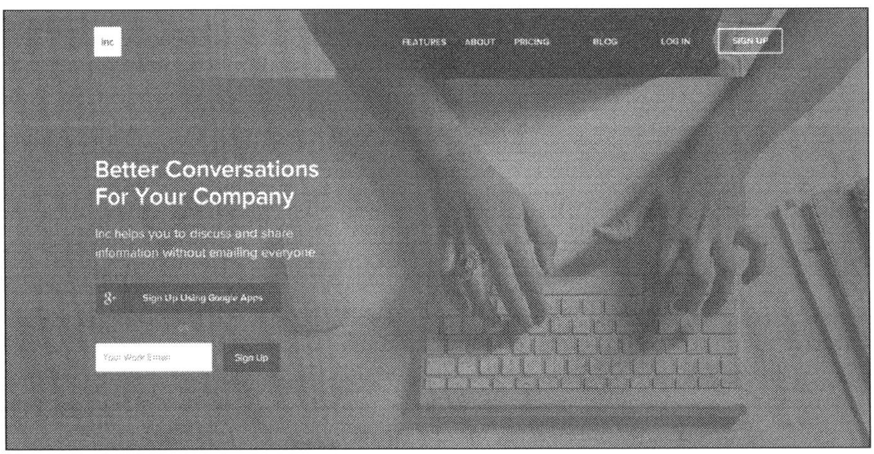

9. Since this is a one-page website, you might be wondering why we're using a menu at all. However, a menu is essential for a website, as it serves as the main navigation tool, and it also tells the viewer which content he or she will be able to find on the website. Since we're creating all our sections on just one page, this menu won't link to different pages, but we are able to scroll down to a specific section using JavaScript. This is how we will lead the viewers to the section that they are looking for. We'll talk more about this, the development of the code, and the technical side of it in *Chapter 5, Developing Your Site*.

10. Now we're going to create our `About` section. Start by creating the title with the font type Lato, font style Bold, and a text size of 40 px. All the words should be in uppercase to maintain consistency. Let's use `About Me` to make the tone a bit more personal. Change the color of the text to `#222222`, to avoid using pure black. This will make it easier on the eyes.
11. Next, create our content. We'll create two text areas and populate them with our text. If you don't have text, you can generate and grab a couple of "lorem ipsum" paragraphs from `http://lipsum.com` to populate the text areas. These two blocks will be 500 px wide each and have a spacing of 35 px between them. Set the text type to Lato, font style to Regular, and text size to 14 px. Also, to make the text more readable and make the columns more visually geometrical, let's select the **Justify last left** option in paragraph options. We'll also set the leading to 20 px.
12. To finish off our `About` section, let's open the `Designmodo flat-ui-free.psd` file. There you will find premade buttons that we can use, so duplicate the `Button` (static) folder to our document and position it below the text areas, centered with the page. Make sure you change the background color of the button to match the color that we selected earlier. Change the copy to `Download Resume`, and this section is completed. The following screenshot is a great example of how you can create visual blocks by just using content:

13. Next is the work section. For this one, let's start by creating eight 225 x 140 px rectangles and align them with 47 px of spacing between them. Create a 2 x 4 grid with these, which will serve as containers for our project's thumbnails. Using thumbnails is an easy and quick way to show your projects. You can opt to use a lightbox plugin such as lightbox 2, which is available at `http://lokeshdhakar.com/projects/lightbox2/`, to show a larger image, or just link it directly to the entry in dribble.
14. To create a visual separation of this block and to contrast with the other sections, let's set a background color for this block. However, instead of using the header color, which is too vivid and bright, let's use a lighter shade of the main color (`#99cbed`). This will create a smoother background that will allow the thumbnails to contrast more with the background. The following screenshot shows the final result:

15. Now, use these rectangles as clipping masks and populate the thumbnails with your work projects. I grabbed a couple of entries from `http://dribbble.com` to populate this example. Again, we want the content to create the visual blocks, so we won't create any kind of borders, lines, or divisions. The way in which we organize content in the grid will be enough to set the visual blocks and define this section's layout.

16. Our work section is now done. You can use titles above or below the thumbnails, but this is a simpler way of doing a work section, and it also shows that your work speaks for itself. By reducing the amount of elements on the page, we're also focusing on creating a minimalistic page, and it's impressive how simple a website can become while reducing the amount of superfluous elements in it. The following screenshot is a good example of a minimalistic page:

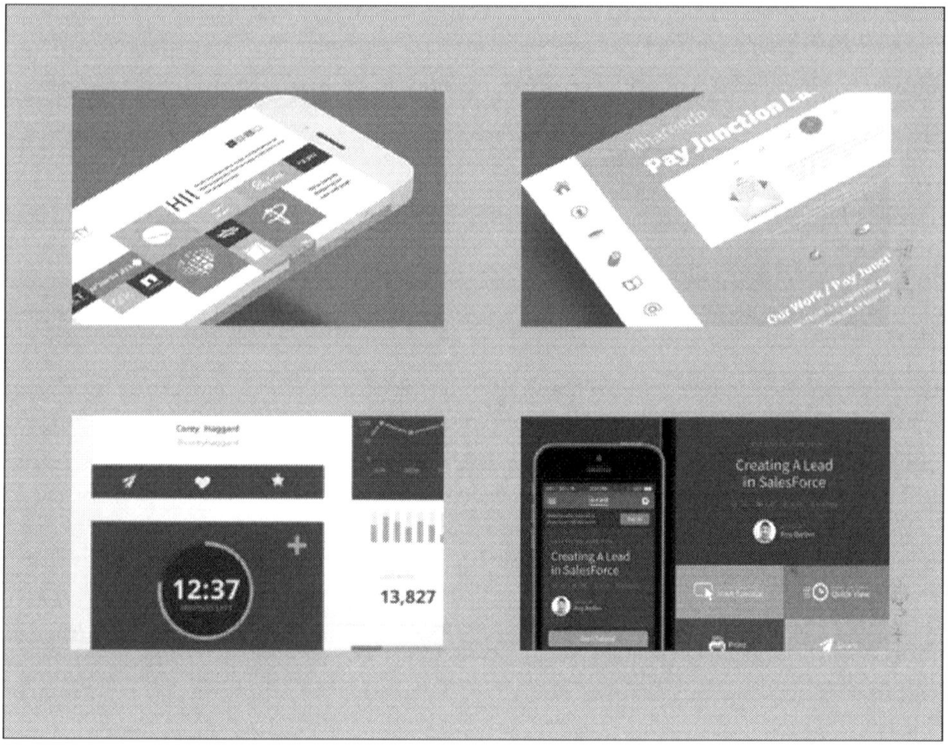

17. Our `Contacts` section is also going to be really simple and minimal. There are several ways of creating `Contact` sections. Usually, you can build a contact form and show a map of of your location and use icons to represent different types of contacts. However, we will go down to the bare basics: a call to action the title, an e-mail address, and a phone number. So, let's duplicate the `About` section's title and change it to `Let's Chat`. Using this kind of text creates a more personal approach to your viewers, as well as represents you as being more approachable, reminding the viewer that this is, in fact, a person who can be easily contacted.

18. After the title, create two text fields in two different lines to add your e-mail address and your phone number. The content of this section will be simple contact information. For these fields, use lowercase text and set the font type to Lato, font style to regular, and font size to 23 px. Using a simple type like this on top of a flat color, we're focusing on the content and impact of the content in itself, as there's nothing else, such as boxes, lines, icons, or maps, to detract it. Flat design is very much composed by this simplicity, focusing on what's essential and the bare minimum. You should be able to see the result, which is similar to the following screenshot:

19. With our `Contact` section done, we're only missing our footer to finish up the website. We'll create a small rectangle (50 px high) for the background and make it the same blue (our main color, `#3498db`) as the header. In here, we will simply ADD our copyright text and the social network icons linked to your accounts. So, create a text field and set the font type to Lato, font style to Bold, and font size to 12 px, with the `© 2014 Designer Name` text. Align this to the left.

20. On the right-hand side of the footer, let's add links to your Twitter and Facebook accounts so that people can connect with you. You can find social logo packs with these links, or you can get the official logos from the brand assets section at `https://www.facebookbrand.com/` for Facebook and `https://about.twitter.com/press/brand-assets` for Twitter. Since we're using our main color as the footer background, let's use the white versions of these logos to make them visible on top of the blue background. Align both of them to the right of the page. It should look like the following screenshot:

The footer is the last element of the website. It serves as a place to add relevant links such as social network links and copyright messaging that are general to the page. It also serves as a visual closure of the site, and it creates the contact section block by visually contrasting between blue and white.

Now that our website is completed, we can review the colors and element's position. It's always easier to make these kind of adjustments and decisions after the layout is constructed, as you're able to visualize all the elements joined together and how they look. In the end, the final choices and touches are mainly to enhance the website's look and feel. Spacing, color, and text make sure that by looking at a website as a whole, you'll feel that it works well, instead of focusing on individual sections.

Our first flat design page is now done, and the whole website should look similar to the following screenshot:

Summary

In this chapter, we covered all the process of designing a single page flat website, from planning, sketching, to final designing in Photoshop, as well as using external resources such as the Designmodo.com Flat UI pack. We were able to design a simple flat website for a designer portfolio, with all the essential sections. In the next chapter, we'll cover the development of the site we just designed using the Designmodo Flat UI pack, HTML, and CSS.

5
Developing Your Site

In this chapter, we'll be developing the flat website we designed in *Chapter 4, Designing Your Own Flat Website*. We will use the Designmodo Flat UI for this, which was created on top of Twitter Bootstrap, a frontend framework that has predeveloped components that allow a quicker development. We will also cover the usage of jQuery to build our navigation animation.

Creating our folder tree

Properly organizing your files, as well as creating a comprehensive file structure, is very important when working in big projects. In smaller projects, you might not realize the importance of this, but it's a habit you should build from the beginning, so that when you work on bigger projects, you implement good practices from the beginning.

This is extremely easy to do, and it's also something you can adapt to your personal taste. I like to keep my files organized in categories. When I begin a development project, one of the first things I like to do is create three folders: `css`, where I obviously keep my CSS style files; `img`, where I save the images used to build the website, and `js`, where I keep all my JavaScript files. In the root of your main folder, you should have your HTML files in a way that you can easily load the rest of your files by using relative paths.

This is a very simple task, but it helps you organize all your files in a way that lets you use relative paths, work locally, and export everything to your server more easily by the end of the project.

A typical folder tree for a web development project will look similar to what is shown in the following screenshot:

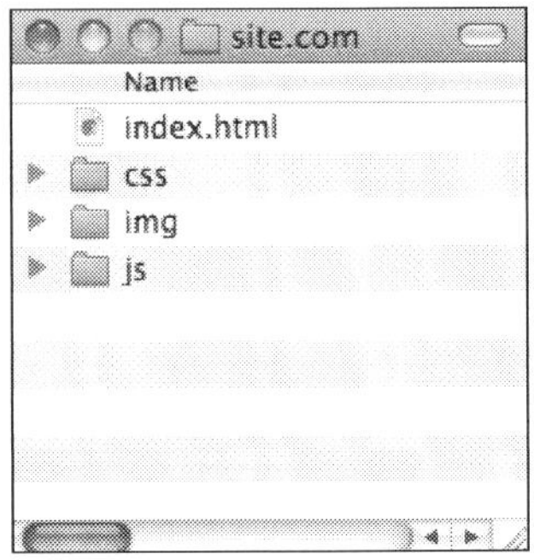

Now that we covered how we're going to start our project, let's get down to business. But before we start the development of our project, we need to get our images ready.

Prepping our images

The first step of our development project is based in Photoshop. We need to go back to our website design file and export the images we need for our page.

Since we designed such a minimal page, most of the elements in our page are made by HTML elements, not by images. We still have a couple of images though, such as our avatar and work thumbnails, so let's export them to use them in our page.

Regarding the avatar, there are two ways that we can go about doing this; the easy way and the proper way. The easy way is to just export our circle avatar and its border as a `.png` file with a transparent background. The following screenshot shows the `Avatar.png` file with a transparent background:

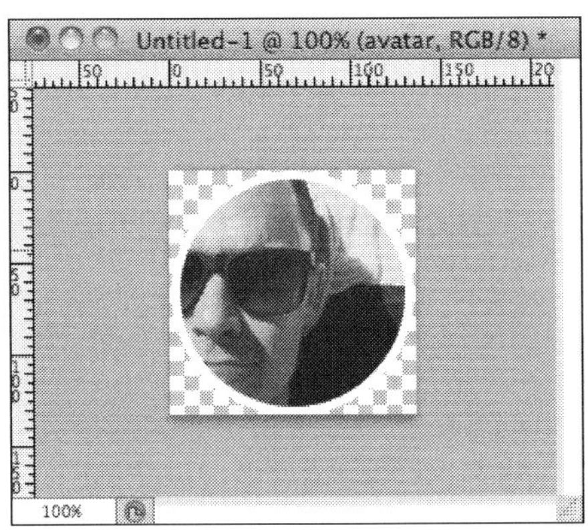

By exporting a transparent `.png` file, we can easily use the image in the web page with any background color, which will work and is probably good enough. But this is not the best way to go about doing this. What if you want to change your avatar after the website is done? Or what if you want to update the website colors and change your stroke color? You will then need to go back to Photoshop and export this image all over again, and that is just a pain.

But luckily enough, we can make most of the effects in HTML, so that you can use just a regular-squared image for the avatar, and let the rest be done by code. This way, you will be able to update your avatar by just changing the regular avatar image or a couple of lines of CSS. Also, if you are doing this project for a client or a company, you are simplifying the updates in the future by making the updates independent of designer work. We will visit the code for this a bit further on in the book; for now, just make sure you export your avatar as a 128 x 128 px square image. This should look similar to what is shown in the following screenshot:

Now, let's export our thumbnails. This part is pretty easy; just make sure you export all the thumbnails with the same size to keep it consistent as well as easier to update in the future. There are several ways of doing this. I like to create a new document with the image dimension (225 x 141 px), copy and paste all my layers there, and save them individually. Then, I save that document as a template for any future usage. This way, I know that every time I need to create a thumbnail, I'll just use that same document.

However, you can use other methods for this. You can use slices and create slices (keyboard shortcut C) for each one of your images in the document, and export the sliced images directly (on the **Save for Web & Devices** menu, you can select the type of slices you'd like to export). You can also use the new feature in Photoshop called **Generate image assets**, available since 2013 in Photoshop CC, which allows you to easily rename a layer or folder to a filename (such as `background.png`), and then just choose to automatically generate an image file from that layer. This is a good way of creating several assets for a big project, and it's very easy to update because the assets are generated automatically with any file saving option. If you're interested in knowing more about image assets generator, I definitely recommend that you should refer to the Adobe Help link: `http://helpx.adobe.com/photoshop/using/generate-assets-layers.html`.

Anyway, you can go on doing this if you want, but make sure that you maintain consistency on your image size and that you export them with 100 percent opacity, because if you're thinking of possibly using any kind of rollover effect, we can and will do it with CSS later on.

The only other two images we're missing are the Twitter and Facebook icons. For these, we'll save them as 32 x 32 px square transparent `.png`, so that we can still use them if we ever wish to change the background of the footer.

We are now done with our image prepping!

Developing our page

Now that we have our images ready, let's start creating our page. Just like with the design, we'll create from top to bottom, starting in the header and developing the layout down to the footer.

We are going to be using Designmodo Flat UI Free for this, so the first thing we need to do is to import the files we're going to use. If you haven't done it already, download this from `http://designmodo.com/flat-free/`. Visit the page and click on **Download HTML**. This will get you a ZIP file with the Designmodo Flat UI Free pack, Twitter Bootstrap 3, and some example files.

So, just as we covered earlier, let's start by creating our folder tree. Create the following folders: `css`, `js`, and `img`. We will also need extra resources, so create two extra folders: `fonts`, where we will save the custom fonts used and `bootstrap`, where we will save the bootstrap files we're going to be using.

Designmodo Flat UI Free pack is built on top of Twitter Bootstrap, so we will effectively be using Twitter Bootstrap to build this page. Twitter Bootstrap is a frontend framework that comes with a variety of predeveloped elements and styles, which makes it easier and quicker for a developer to create simple pages. I am a firm believer of optimizing work, and there's no need to be continuously reinventing the wheel. Most of the things we're going to use have been done hundreds or millions of times, so let's make use of the common effort to make our own lives easier. Here's when Twitter Bootstrap comes really handy. If you want to learn more about Twitter Bootstrap and see all the examples and guides, you can do so online at `http://getbootstrap.com/`.

Now that we have our file structure created, let's populate it with the needed files. First up, let's upload the images we previously exported from Photoshop into the `img` folder. In our `css` folder, we'll paste the `flat-ui.css` file from the Designmodo pack. We won't be using any JavaScript for now, so we don't need to copy the JavaScript files provided in the pack. Copy the content of the Designmodo pack's `fonts` folder into your own `fonts` folder, and copy the `bootsrap` folder as well and paste it in your `root` folder. This includes all the styles and resources used by Bootstrap. By now, your main folder should look similar to what is shown in the following screenshot:

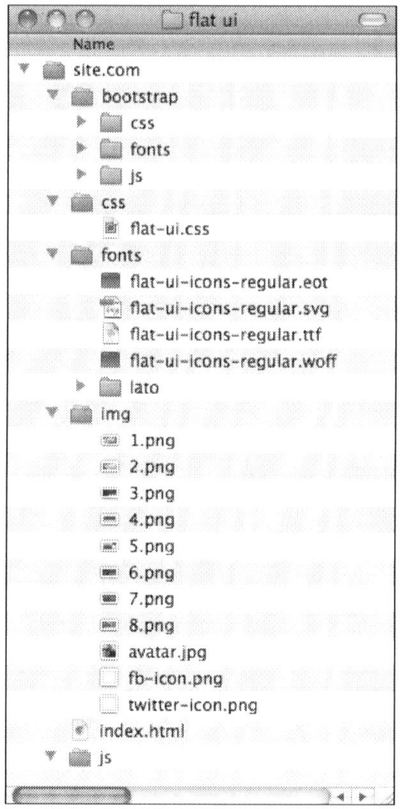

This includes all the required files to start creating our page, and with these in place, we can finally start the HTML.

Open your HTML editor and create a new file called `index.html`. This will be our website. The Designmodo pack has a file called `template.html`, which is a clean starter page with the basic HTML structure already initialized, which is a good foundation to work on. So open the file, copy its content, and paste it into your `index.html` file.

The following screenshot shows what you should have on your index file:

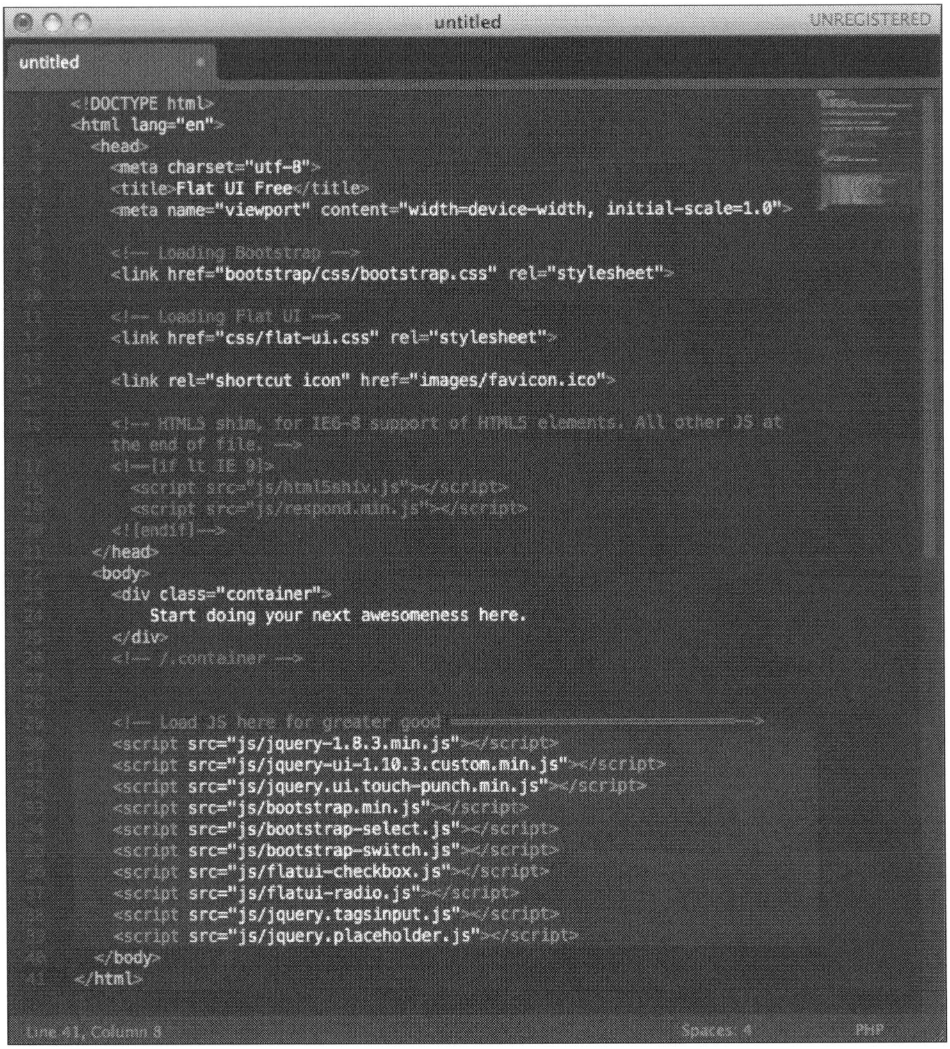

We can delete some content from here. The favicon part, `<link rel="shortcut icon" href="images/favicon.ico">`, can be deleted as we didn't design a favicon for this page, as well as for all the scripts being loaded after `<!-- Load JS here for greater good =============================-->`. We will be using JavaScript, but we will be loading the files as we need them to avoid having unnecessary files occupying space.

We won't be creating any CSS file for now; we will only focus on creating the HTML file and getting the document with the content ready to style it afterwards. As we are using Twitter Bootstrap, we'll try to replicate our design as best as possible just by using existing features and styles from Bootstrap, and only after that can we create our own styles to customize the page to our needs.

So, to create our header, we will need a `<div>` element that will fill the whole browser in width to create that visual effect we designed. To do this, we will be using a class called `jumbotron` that Bootstrap already provides. You can see the example Bootstrap file online at `http://getbootstrap.com/examples/jumbotron/`. Essentially, this is a `div` class, the width of which is defined as 100 percent and stretches to fill the browser with a different background color. The structure for this `div` is as follows:

```
<div class="jumbotron">
      <div class="container">
      </div>
    </div>
```

Insert this code right after the `<body>` tag. If you save and refresh your file in the browser, you'll be able to see the effect of the layer filling the browser in the `Jumbotron` div. Now, we just need to insert our content inside the `div` container, as shown in the following code:

```
<p class="text-center" ><img src="img/avatar.jpg"/></p>
        <p class="text-center">
            <a href="#">About</a>
            <a href="#">Work</a>
            <a href="#">Contacts</a>
        </p>
```

As you can see, we're using `class="text-center"` in some of our elements. This is a Bootstrap class responsible to set the text alignment to be centered, and it will center our elements, making this look a bit like our design header. Granted, there are some things changes to be made, but we will make these changes afterwards in CSS. The following screenshot shows how our HTML file looks when we open it in the browser:

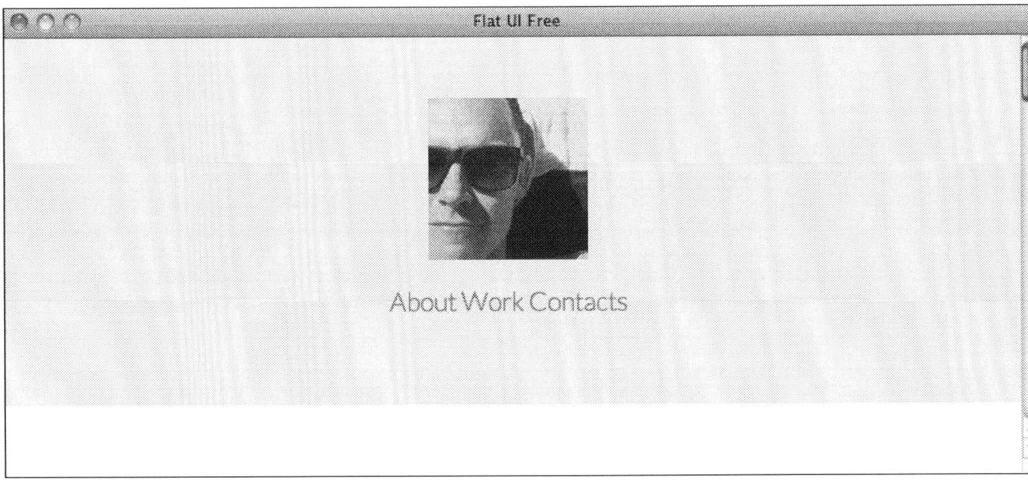

Pretty close to what we're looking to do, right?

Now, for our `About` section, we will need to create a title, two blocks of text, and a button. Luckily enough, this is also mostly done by using Bootstrap styles. For the title, we will use an `<h2>` tag; for the blocks, we will use a paragraph with a specific block class, which will look like this: `<div class="col-md-6">`. Twitter Bootstrap comes with a responsive grid system implemented, which is composed of 12 columns. So in this case, we want to create two blocks that will occupy each half of the screen. So, every block will have six columns, hence the class `col-md-6` is used. As I said, this is a responsive grid, which means that the website will adapt to tablets and smartphones by dynamically resizing the columns' sizes to fit the devices used.

Our button is also easily implemented by using Bootstrap tags; in this case, it is the flat style, due to the Designmodo Flat UI pack. Our button will look like this: `<p class="text-center"><button class="btn btn-hg btn-primary">Download Resume</button></p>`. The button element has the `btn` class, which is the main class responsible for giving the button its look; the others are to set color and behavior. We will change this afterwards to use our color and font options. So, the HTML code for this section is as follows:

```
<div class="container">
   <div class="row">
```

```
        <h2 class="text-center">About Me</h2>
        <div class="col-md-6">
          <p>Text</p>
        </div>
        <div class="col-md-6">
          <p>Text</p>
        </div>
       <p class="text-center">
          <button class="btn btn-hg btn-primary">
          Download Resume</button></p>
      </div>
  </div>
```

Just replace the text of our bigger block of text to adapt it to the column; our **About Me** section should look like the following screenshot:

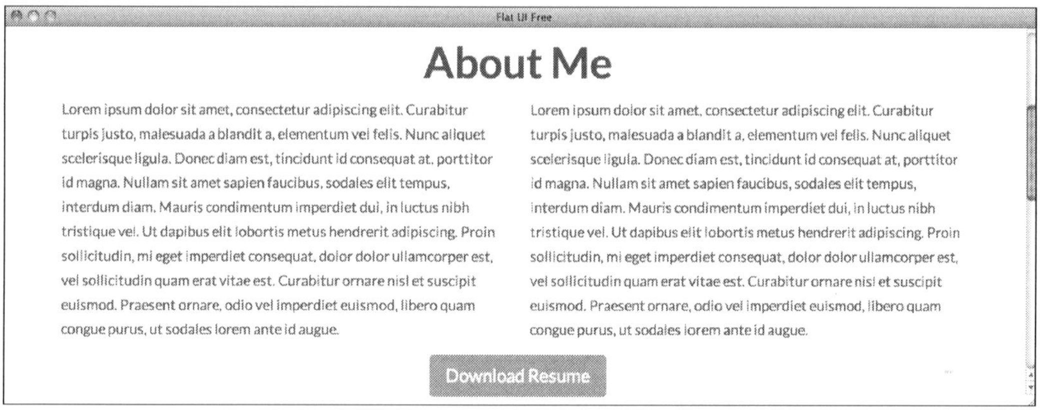

Next, we will create our `Work` section. Since this will also have a blue wide background, we will be using the `jumbotron div` element again for our main container. We have a grid of 2 x 4 thumbnails in our design, and since rows and columns compose the Bootstrap grid, we will need to create two rows, one for each line of four thumbnails. Thinking about the way that the 12-column grid works in Bootstrap, we will need to use *12/4 = 3* columns for each thumbnail, of which we have four. The following is our final code for the work section:

```
<div class="jumbotron">
      <div class="container">
        <div class="row">
          <div class="text-center col-sm-6 col-md-3">
            <img src="img/1.png"/></div>
          <div class="text-center col-sm-6 col-md-3">
            <img src="img/2.png"/></div>
          <div class="text-center col-sm-6 col-md-3">
            <img src="img/3.png"/></div>
```

```
          <div class="text-center col-sm-6 col-md-3">
            <img src="img/4.png"/></div>
        </div>
        <div class="row">
          <div class="text-center col-sm-6 col-md-3">
            <img src="img/5.png"/></div>
          <div class="text-center col-sm-6 col-md-3">
            <img src="img/6.png"/></div>
          <div class="text-center col-sm-6 col-md-3">
            <img src="img/7.png"/></div>
          <div class="text-center col-sm-6 col-md-3">
            <img src="img/8.png"/></div>
        </div>
      </div>
    </div>
```

So, here you can see that we created a `jumbotron div` element for the background, two row `div` elements for our lines, and each row has four divisions with an image inside, which is our thumbnail. It is important to check the classes we used for this `div` element because they are used for grids. The div used, `<div class="text-center col-sm-6 col-md-3">`, has three different classes. The `text-center` class is used to center our image in the block; it's responsive, it will change size depending on the screen size, and we don't want the image to be larger than the original file size, as that will create pixilation and ruin the image quality. The class `col-md-3` is responsible to align the positioning of the images in the grid in desktop devices, meaning that each will occupy three columns. The class `col-sm-6` refers to tablet devices, and it means that in tablet widths, it will show two thumbnails per line. This creates a better adaptive experience as it will show four thumbnails per line on desktops, two on tablets, and only one on smartphones, the smallest of them all, as shown in the following screenshot:

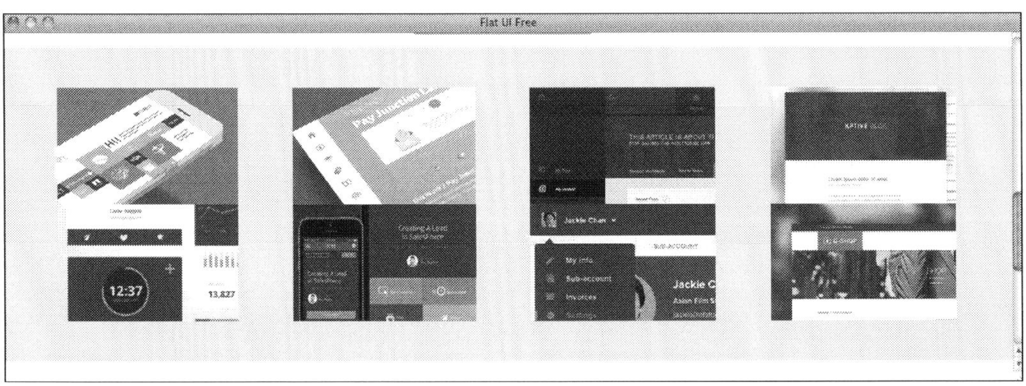

With only the Bootsrap code, we were able to create a responsive grid of thumbnails that we can use for our Work section, quickly and easily.

The Contact section is probably the easiest of them all, as we just need to create three lines of content. We will use a <h2> element for the title again, and then two <p> elements for each line of content, as shown in the following code:

```
<div class="container">
  <h2 class="text-center">Let's Chat</h2>
    <p class="text-center"><a href="mailto:designer@portfolio.
com">designer@portfolio.com</a></p>
  <p class="text-center">+44 1234 567 890</p>
</div>
```

The code is fairly simple as well. We're just using the text-center tag to center the text in the page, and then we're creating a link in the e-mail, so that the visitor can click directly to send any mail. By using href=mailto:designer@portfolio.com, we're allowing the browser to open a mail program to create a new e-mail with the e-mail field already filled with this information, making it easier to send a message. This behavior might not be good in every case, because sometimes the default e-mail program might not be configured, or the user might use a webmail client that won't be able to open this kind of link, so use this only if you believe it makes sense to.

The following screenshot shows how our simple contact section looks:

The last element to create is the footer, and we'll again use the jumbotron div element for this. We will need to make some more adjustments to make sure that the footer sticks to the bottom of the page, but we'll do that in a minute when we work in our page styles.

So, for the footer, we'll create the `jumbotron div` element, a paragraph with our copyright text, and two hyperlinks with the social network icons. This won't look at all like what we're trying to achieve, but our content is there as we need it, and now it's only down to the styles to change the look of it. The following is the final piece of code for our footer:

```
<div class="jumbotron">
      <div class="container">
        <p>
          <span class="text-left">© 2014 Designer Name</span>
          <a href="#"><img src="img/twitter-icon.png"></a>
          <a href="#"><img src="img/fb-icon.png"></a>
        </p>
      </div>
    </div>
```

With this last piece of code, our basic HTML page is done, ready for some styling work with CSS.

Styling our page with CSS

Let's start by creating a new file called `main.css` in the `css` folder. This will be where we will place our own styles to customize the look of the page to our design. With our file in place, we now need to link our CSS file in our HTML page. Go to your `index.html` file and add `<link href="css/main.css" rel="stylesheet">` to the `<head>` tag, and make sure you add it after `bootsrap.css` and `flat-ui.css`; otherwise, our styles might be overridden and won't work.

The first change we'll be making is the text color. As we want it to be the color we set in our design, let's set the text color to `#222222` for every element in the `<body>` tag. We do this by using the following code:

```
body{
  color: #222222;
}
```

Now, let's start with the header, let's make its background blue. The color code we will choose for this is `#3498db`, and since we want to change this for every `jumbotron div` element, we'll target the `jumbotron` class, as shown in the following code:

```
.jumbotron{
  background-color: #3498db;
}
```

Save the file and refresh it in the browser, and you'll notice that it will immediately look a lot more like your design with the blue background sections. For the avatar, I told you before that we could do the circle avatar in CSS. We're able to do this because of CSS3, which allows us to easily create rounded corners in borders and border-radius. By setting that border at 50 percent, it will create such a radius in every corner that leads to a perfect circle. So, keep in mind that this won't work in every browser, as not all browsers support CSS3, but you should always use the latest technologies and techniques available to make good use of them, while always keeping in mind a graceful degradation of older versions.

In this case, the only problem is that the avatar will be a square rather than a circle in older browsers. This is not a major problem because it's just a visual difference and it doesn't influence the business or usability at all. But going back to our avatar, we want it as a circle and with a white border, so we need to target our avatar in our CSS selectors. Since our avatar is just an `<img>` tag, we need to go back to the HTML file and change our tag to include a class, such as `<img class="avatar" src="img/avatar.jpg"/>`. Now, we can target `.avatar` in our CSS, and the following is the code we will use for the effects:

```
.avatar{
  -webkit-border-radius: 50%;
  -moz-border-radius: 50%;
  -ms-border-radius: 50%;
  -o-border-radius: 50%;
  border-radius: 50%;
  border: solid 5px #FFF;
  display: inline-block;
}
```

This will do the trick and our avatar will now look exactly like in our original design. However, you might run into some problems with Safari and other browsers, as each browser has slightly different ways of rendering these elements. So, you can make a small change and it will still work. Instead of having the image in your HTML file, you can define it as background image from the CSS, and this will solve the problem. In your HTML file, change the line to `<p class="text-center"><span class="avatar"></span></p>`; in the CSS file, add the following parameters:

```
background: url('../img/avatar.jpg');
height: 128px;
width: 128px;
```

Now, it should work in Safari as well, but every time you try some new technology, make sure to check where it works and breaks, because there's always some way to adapt your code to make it work. The following screenshot shows how your avatar works in live HTML pages:

For the menu, the following is the code we're going to use:

```
#header a{
  text-transform: uppercase;
  color: #ffffff;
  margin: 0 15px 0 15px;
  font-weight: bolder;
}

#menu{
  margin-top:50px;
}
```

> Remember, always indent your code, be it HTML, CSS, JavaScript, or any other language. It makes it easier for you and others to read and to quickly visualize and analyze a bigger chunk of code.

As you can see, we're using new IDs in this CSS. The `#header` class is the ID that we've set in the HTML for the whole header `<div>`, and `#menu` is the ID set for the `<p>` element where we have our menu links. As we start to do more and more styling, we will need to set classes and IDs to be able to select specific elements in the HTML file. Here, we're making sure that our links are uppercase by using `text-transform` and changing the color to white. Also, we're changing the font weight to a heavier weight in order to adapt to our design.

For the About section, we need to change some things, such as the title size, font size of the text, as well as line height. Finally, we'll use margin and padding to make the spacing between elements exactly as we had designed. A really important part of this CSS is the `text-align: justify` property that makes the block of text have the same text alignment as that of our design, shaping the text to fit the block and helping to visually define the layout.

We also want to change the color of the button to match our color palette, so we do that by defining the background color of the `.btn` element. This way we override the color previously used. We will also change the color on mouse rollover, so we will use the selector `.btn:hover` to change the style of the element when the mouse is over it. You will notice that there's a small fade when you rollover the button, and this comes from `css-transitions` being used in the Designmodo Flat UI pack's CSS files, which set this as an effect applied to every link and button. Let's use the following code:

```
#about h2{
  font-size: 35px;
  text-transform: uppercase;
  margin: 70px 0 70px 0;
  color: #222222;
}

#about p.text{
  font-size: 14px;
  line-height: 1.70;
  text-align: justify;
  color: #222222;
}

#about .btn{
  margin-top: 90px;
  margin-bottom: 135px;
  background-color: #3498DB;
  font-size: 17px;
  padding: 12px 40px;
}

#about .btn:hover{
  background-color: #99CBED;
}
```

The following screenshot is how our `About` section looks after setting the CSS:

Our `Work` section doesn't require a lot of changes on the CSS file, as it's already pretty similar to what we're looking to do. So, we'll just change the background color of the `jumbotron div` element, and leave some margin between the elements to make them equally spaced, as shown in the following code:

```
#work{
  background: #99cbed;
  padding-top: 95px;
}

#work img{
  margin-bottom: 50px;
}
```

For our `Contacts` section, our content is composed by an `<h2>` tag, a link, and text for the phone number. This is fairly easy to stylize as well, and it's mostly just color and text size changes, along with a margin setting to adapt to this part. Use the following code for the `Contacts` section:

```
#contacts{
  margin-bottom: 80px;
}

#contacts p{
  font-size: 23px;
}

#contacts h2{
```

```
    font-size: 35px;
    text-transform: uppercase;
    margin: 70px 0 35px 0;
    color: #222222;
  }

  #contacts a{
    color: #222222;
  }

  #contacts a:hover{
    color: #3498db;
  }
```

At last, let's work on our footer. This currently doesn't resemble much of our design, so we need to make it smaller by defining its height, making the text smaller, and aligning our icons to the right. To align our icons, we'll be using `float: right`; we'll use `margin` to create some spacing between the icons. The following is the CSS part of code created for this bit:

```
  #footer{
    height: 50px;
    margin-bottom: 0px;
    padding-top: 25px;
    padding-bottom: 60px;
  }

  #footer span{
    color: #fff;
    font-size: 11px;
  }

  #footer .icon{
    float: right;
    margin-left: 10px;
  }
```

We had to set the class icon for the element `<a href="#" class="icon"><img src="img/fb-icon.png"></a>`, so that we could effectively target just these icons and align them to the right in the same line. This concludes the CSS work for our layout page.

By just using some simple CSS lines to align elements and change some colors, this looks extremely similar to our design. Let's take a look at how our page appears now. It should look similar to what is shown in the following screenshot:

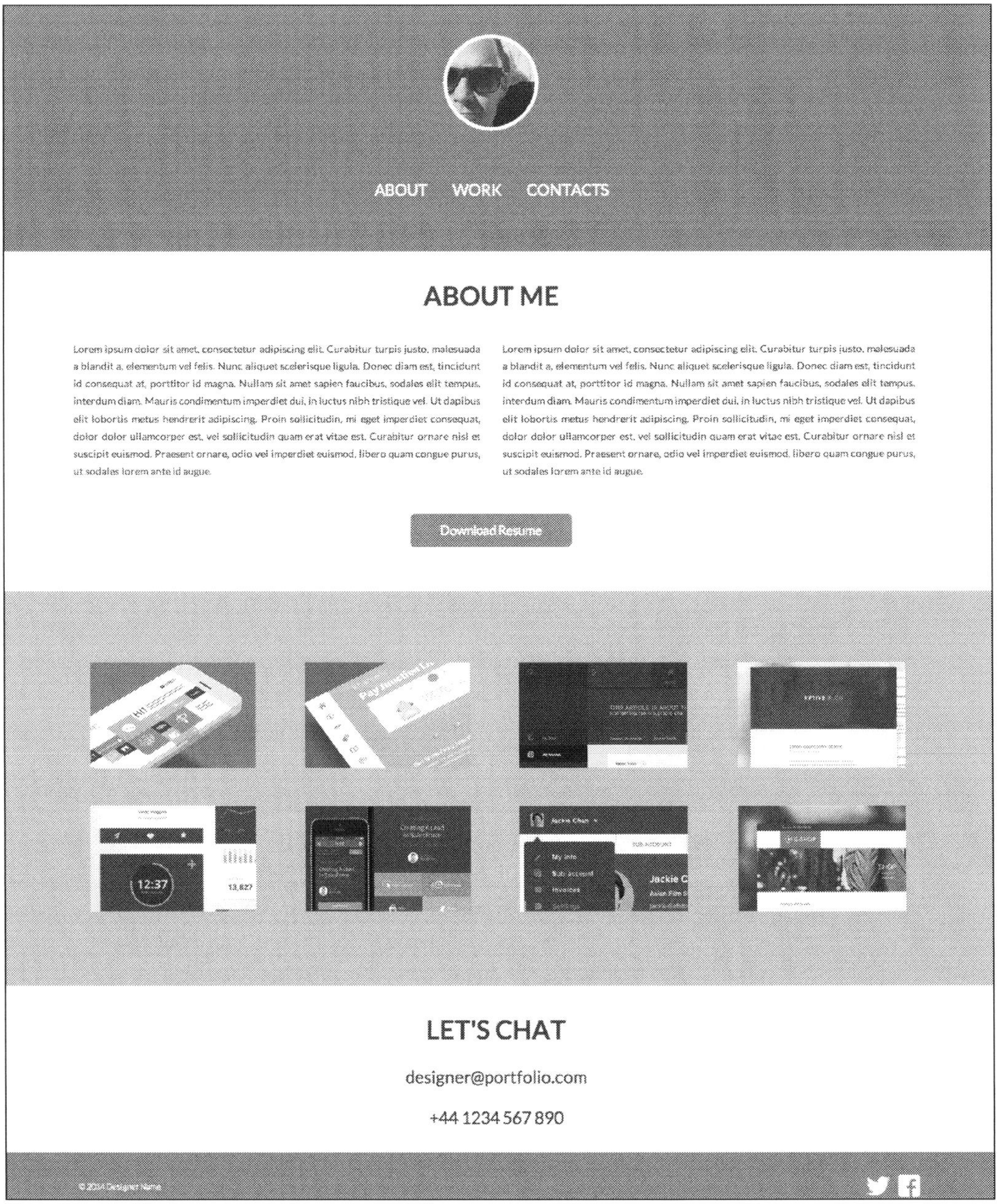

Using jQuery for navigation

As we said before, we can use a slide to the `section` code to create our single page website navigation, so that when the user clicks in the menu, the page scrolls to the beginning of that section. To accomplish that effect, we will be using a jQuery plugin called `PageScroller`, available at `http://pagescroller.com/`. There are two versions: Pro and Lite. For this exercise, the Lite version will be enough, as we only need the minimum functionality. The way we're going to implement this is extremely easy as well, but if you're looking for more options, you can check the plugin `readme` file and the website.

First of all, we'll need to load the JavaScript files needed for this. After unpacking the plugin, copy and paste the `jquery.pagescroller.lite.js` file into your `js` folder. We will also need jQuery for this, but we will load it from the **Content Delivery Network (CDN)** from an external path. So, include these two lines in your `<head>` element, ideally before the `</head>` tag, as shown in the following code:

```
<script type="text/javascript"
src="http://code.jquery.com/jquery-latest.min.js"></script>
<script type="text/javascript"
src="js/jquery.pagescroller.lite.js"></script>
```

This will load the JavaScript files to your page, but you will now need to initialize the plugin.

You can do this by simply calling the function `pageScroller()` inside a `document.ready` JavaScript function, which means that it will only be started after our document is loaded. Take a look at the following code:

```
<script type="text/javascript">
$(document).ready(function(){
  // initiate page scroller plugin
  $('body').pageScroller({
    navigation: '#menu'
  }); });
</script>
```

With the script loaded and initialized, everything is ready to go. So, the way that the plugin works is listening to clicks on the element specific when initialized, that in this case we defined as our `#menu div` element in `navigation: '#menu'`. Now, it will look for the `class` section to scroll to it, so we need to add this class to our titles.

Ideally, we want to add this to either the beginning of our container or our <h2> title for the section. The following code shows how we have defined the sections in our HTML document:

```
<div id="about" class="container section">
      <div class="row">
(..)
<div id="work" class="jumbotron section">
(..)
<div id="contacts" class="container section">
```

This way, we're targeting the beginning of our sections each time by adding the class section to it, and when clicking in the menu, it will scroll the page to the corresponding section. Try it out, and you'll see that it scrolls directly to the section clicked in the menu.

This kind of navigation works even better with bigger sections, but it's a quick and easy way to add a cool and easy navigation to our single-page website.

Summary

This is it for our development! In this chapter, we developed our single-page website by using the Designmodo Flat UI pack to simplify the workflow. We put organization of files, image exporting, and project phases in practice, and we learned how to approach a project and what you should have in mind in bigger projects. We also had our first interaction with Twitter Bootstrap, which is the foundation of the Flat UI pack. We managed to create a very similar look to our layout by just using HTML, predefined Bootstrap classes, and custom CSS styles to create the exact design we've done before. We also used `PageScroller` to create our single-page scroll navigation.

Next, let's see how we can create our own Flat UI kit by creating our own components.

6
Creating Your Own Flat UI Kit

In this last chapter, we'll learn how you can create your own personal Flat UI kit. We will cover all phases of the process, from designing to developing and exporting your assets. These are the most important elements that you need to bear in mind while creating your own pack. We will also explain how to ensure ease of use for you or anyone else by documenting every element and usage.

Designing your components

To create your own Flat UI pack, the first step is to define which elements you should create. Your objective is to create and gather a pack of elements to reuse in future projects, so you should look for basic interface elements that are common to most projects. Elements such as buttons, form controls such as radio buttons and checkboxes, form content areas such as text fields and text areas, title style, and sizes such as `<h1>`, `<h2>`, and `<h3>`, once designed, thought of, and developed, can be reused in several projects. Often, a web designer finds himself or herself reusing old HTML and CSS code, so creating your own personal pack is great in order to make your workflow easier and quicker.

The first phase of creating your own Flat UI pack is to design your elements. There are several designs online for UI packs, web elements, and even great icon packs that you can use as an inspiration for your own work. A simple search on `dribbble.com` will help you find great elements that you can use as inspiration, or even some freebies that you can use as a foundation to create your own designs.

The following screenshot shows an example of a Flat UI pack by Alexandre Crenn at `http://dribbble.com/shots/1020321-FREE-Pack-UI-PSD`:

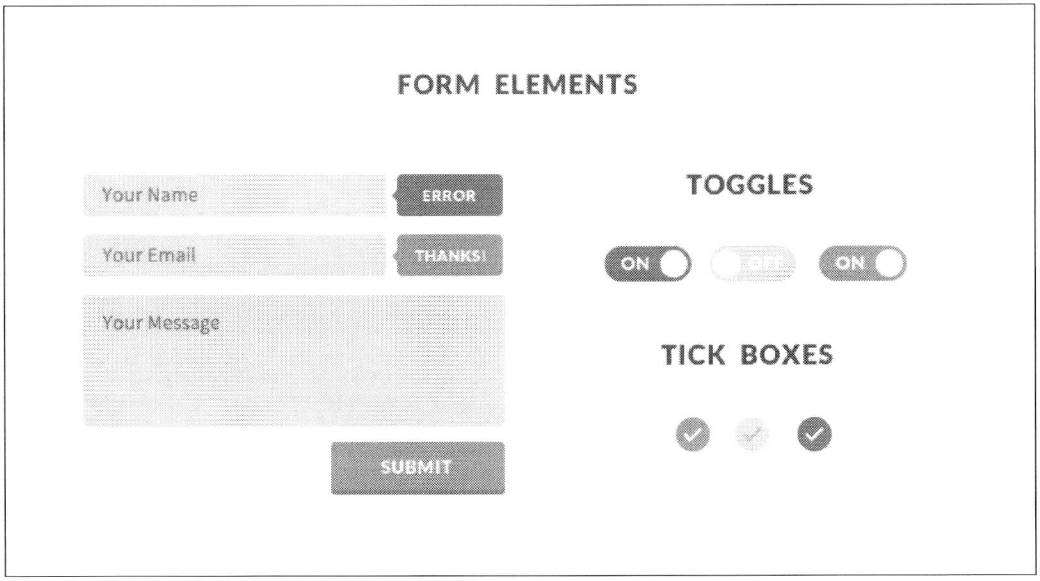

To create your pack, define what elements you want to include and design. Make a list of the elements you need most and that you will be working on, and then start designing them.

As an example, let's do an exercise and create one of those elements for your personal pack. Let's create a button, as it's one of the most used and more visually impactful elements of them all, by executing the following steps:

1. Open Photoshop and create a new 320 by 95 px document.
2. Using the rounded rectangle tool, create a rectangle with 8 px of radius and `#2ecc71` as the background color. The output will be similar to what is shown in the following screenshot:

3. Let's create a more interesting flat button this time and give it some depth. Duplicate this layer, change its color to `#27ae60`, and move it 5 px down. Make sure that this second rectangle is under the first one that we've created in the layer order. This makes the second rectangle appear as a side of the button along with its shadow. Only by making this slight change, you'll be able to see that we have a depth effect in the button, as shown in the following screenshot:

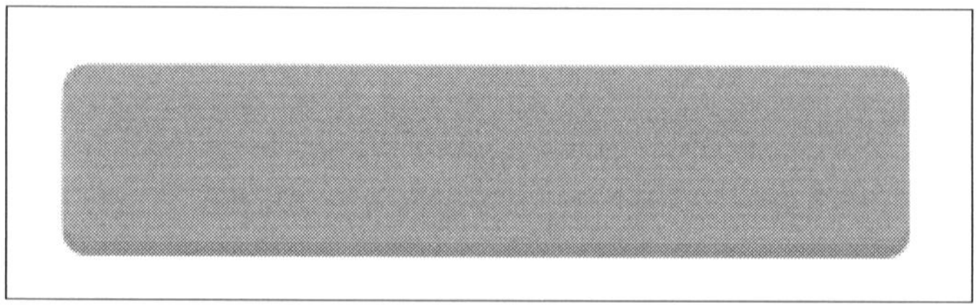

4. To finish designing our button, let's create a text field with `CLICK HERE` written on it. Use type face Lato, font style white, and set the size as 20 pt. Now, create a drop shadow layer style in the text layer with 1 px of distance and 1 px of size, color black with 33 percent opacity.
5. Now, our new flat button is complete, as shown in the following screenshot:

As you can see, we used a drop shadow in the text and a 3D depth effect in this flat button. You might be wondering about this, as I had previously spoken against the use of such effects. The truth is that you can use a drop shadow and even a 3D object, such as the one used in the preceding image, as long as you're able to use them wisely and in a subtle way. This button, even with a drop shadow and depth, still looks flat, and looks definitely more appealing with this kind of characteristics. However, it is, in essence, still a flat button, and not a direct representation of a physical button. Also, the drop shadow is very subtle in the text, just enough to pop the text a bit. As with everything, don't be too harsh with the rules; try to experiment with the style and see what works best. However, to achieve minimalism, you need to be able to focus on the essentials and design clean elements.

Now that we have designed our button, we are ready to translate this into code. As this button can be entirely created in HTML and CSS, thanks to CSS3 border-radius and text-shadow features, we don't need to do any image exporting. However, in a different element, say a radio button or a checkbox, we would need to prepare those images. So, we move on to the next step, that is, exporting images and coding your elements.

Exporting and coding

As I said before, this step is where you would export and prepare any images needed for your pack. There are a few different ways of dealing with images. Be it an icon or a background, you should try to optimize your images as best as possible. A great way to reduce the size of images and speed up the loading of a page is by using CSS Sprites. Sprites were originally used for video games where a single image file would have several frames of an animation, which were then loaded, and changing the coordinates of the image shown would create the animation, just like in a traditional animation. The following screenshot shows Super Mario Bros. 3 Sprite Sheets:

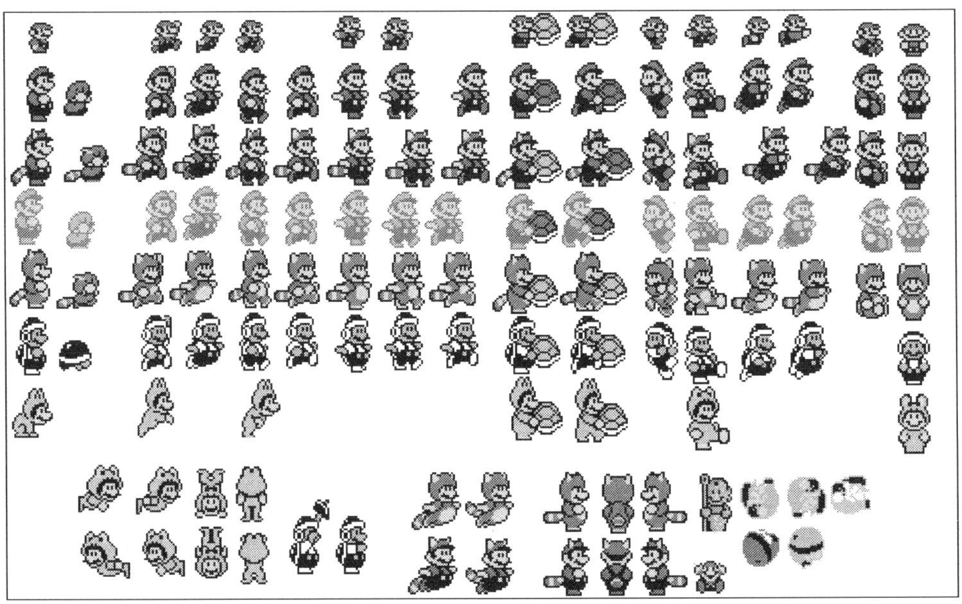

This same technique is used for web and interface designs, by creating buttons, icons, and several states, and including them in just a single image, and then using CSS to show only the portion that we need for a certain element. There are programs and online applications that can be very helpful to create the CSS code for those Sprites, which is a lot quicker than calculating them and creating all the CSS code manually. Online applications such as Sprite Cow (`http://www.spritecow.com/`) and software such as Sprite Right (`http://spriterightapp.com/`) are extremely helpful to create CSS Sprites, and you should definitely take a look at them and try using sprites in your next big project. For now, let's go back to our button. The following screenshot shows sprites from Amazon.com:

Since our button is made up of only code, we can go directly into development without the need to export any image for this element. So let's jump straight to our code editor and perform the following steps:

1. Let's first create the HTML code for our button. We'll need to create a simple HTML page just to host the button. Create a new HTML file named `button.html` with the following code as reference:

```
<!DOCTYPE html>
<html lang="en">
<head>
</head>
<body>
<button class="btn">Click Here</button>
</body>
</html>
```

Here, you can see that our button is effectively a `<button>` element, with the class `class="nbtn"`. It is good to use small names for classes as they are small and easy to recognize and write. While developing your pack, you want to think as much as you can about how you can reuse your CSS. So for instance, while creating a button, if you want to create several colors of the same button, you should create a class `btn` and then a class for each color, such as red, blue, and so on. This way, the `btn` class would have only the CSS for the sizing and appearance, and you would define the color in a separate class. This means that you'd be reusing the class `btn` for every kind of color, making it easier to customize and change it for future usage. A red button would then look like `<button class=tbtn redred class=then look l>`. It's just a matter of thinking of how you can mix different classes for different objectives when creating your CSS.

2. Let's get back to our button. Now that we created our HTML file, if you open the file in a browser, you'll see our button completely unstyled, with the default browser look. So, with the HTML file created, it's time for us to style this element with CSS. First of all, we want to use a custom font for this, so include this line in the `<head>` element of your HTML file: `<link href='http://fonts.googleapis.com/css?family=Lato:700' rel='stylesheet' type='text/css'>`. This will load the typeface Lato to be used in our button. For the sake of organization, we'll create our CSS code in our header, so create a `<style></style> element inside the <head>`.
3. To create the look of a button, the following is the CSS code that we're going to use:

```
.btn{
-moz-border-radius: 8px;
-webkit-border-radius: 8px;
border-radius: 8px;
border:none;
border-bottom: 5px solid #27ae60;
background: #2ecc71;
font-family: 'Lato', sans-serif;
text-shadow: 0 1px 2px #239a55;
font-size: 20px;
color: #ffffff;
height: auto;
margin: 0;
width: 210px;
display: block;
padding: 15px;
text-transform: uppercase;
width: 250px;
float: left;
outline: none;
}
```

So, going over the code, we're defining the border-radius as 8 px, and unfortunately, due to browser compatibilities, we have to include several browser prefixes to make sure that it will work in most browsers. We're not only setting the background color to our chosen green, but also setting the color and typeface of the text as well as its shadow.

4. If you refresh your browser now, you'll see that the design we used previously is now completely developed, including the 3D depth. This was done by creating a bigger bottom border with `border-bottom: 5px solid #27ae60`. We've given the border a radius of 5 px and a darker shade of green, creating the illusion of depth to the button. The last part, `outline: none`, is also very important as it's the one that deactivates the browser focus outline, which is usually a blue glow or a blue border (depending on the browser used). So this way, we make sure that our element doesn't have any other kind of effect applied, other than the ones created by us.

   The following shows us how the button looks now with our CSS:

> A great resource to create your CSS3 code is `css3generator.com`. It lets you fine-tune and visualize details such as border radius and box shadows. It is great for helping you deal with several browser-specific prefixes.

Now, for the different states, our button has the following properties that are used in this code:

```
.btn:hover{
outline: none;
border: 1px solid #27ae60;
margin-top:3px;
}


.btn:active{
outline: none;
padding-top: 16px;
padding-bottom: 14px;
-webkit-box-shadow: inset 0px 0px 5px 0px rgba(0, 0, 0, 1);
box-shadow: inset 0px 0px 5px 0px rgba(0, 0, 0, 1);
}
```

The `.btn:hover` class is the rollover effect that occurs when the mouse is over the button. What we're aiming to do is to make it appear as if the button is being pressed, so we're changing the border to a smaller one in order to give a sort of shadow to the button, and losing the bigger border-bottom. However, since the button needs to go down, we give it a margin-top of 3 px to make it look like the button is really being pressed down, as shown in the following screenshot:

For the active state, when the button is clicked, we want to make it look like it's been pressed down from its previous state. So, we're creating an inset shadow and changing the padding to make the text go down a couple of pixels, just enough to make the user feel like it's physically going down a bit. While interacting with it, you understand the effect it creates and how well it works. The following screenshot shows the button in the active state:

This is it for the development of our button! It's ready to be used in your pack and in future projects. You can always customize it further and create different sizes for it based on the same kind of appearance.

Documentation is key

When you're creating your elements and your scripts, you should document everything. Organization and documentation is extremely important so that you can properly reuse the elements that you create. Also, if you're working with more people on a regular basis, you should make sure that all your classes have understandable names. Also, make sure to comment your CSS as well as your HTML in such a way that anyone else can just grab and use your code in the future. Sometimes, it so happens that bad names for classes are used, and when you're looking for a specific class or trying to understand your code, it can be a really daunting task without any kind of support or documentation.

The best way to make sure that all your code is understandable is to use comments. In HTML, you can do that by using the enclosing code or text comments as follows:

```
<!-- This is a HTML comment.-->
```

In CSS, you can also comment code or add your own text as follows:

```
/* This is a CSS Comment */
```

These can and should be used as much as possible. Be concise and describe exactly what your code does, as in the future, you or anyone else will revisit it and will need to get an understanding of the function and objective. You can also use comments to timestamp changes and author in order to keep track of the last updates on a file.

In the case of bigger and more complex projects, you can create complete `readme` files, with textual guides that explain the elements and how to design them. However, comments are usually enough for this and are easier as they are placed directly in the working files.

Summary

In this chapter, we covered the process of creating your own Flat UI pack, from element design to development, and also elaborated on how to create documentation and comment your work for future use. We created a flat design button in CSS to exemplify a process and create one asset of the pack.

This is also the last chapter, and with it, we come to the end of our book. Here, we covered all the phases of a web design project in flat design, focusing on the specifics of the flat style and how it's so easy and impactful to create projects. From planning, sketching, and designing, up until development, you're now ready to create your own page, and you just need to go ahead and put this in practice, because the more you practice, the better you'll become.

Index

[PACKT] open source
community experience distilled
PUBLISHING

Thank you for buying

Creating Flat Design Websites

About Packt Publishing

Packt, pronounced 'packed', published its first book "*Mastering phpMyAdmin for Effective MySQL Management*" in April 2004 and subsequently continued to specialize in publishing highly focused books on specific technologies and solutions.

Our books and publications share the experiences of your fellow IT professionals in adapting and customizing today's systems, applications, and frameworks. Our solution based books give you the knowledge and power to customize the software and technologies you're using to get the job done. Packt books are more specific and less general than the IT books you have seen in the past. Our unique business model allows us to bring you more focused information, giving you more of what you need to know, and less of what you don't.

Packt is a modern, yet unique publishing company, which focuses on producing quality, cutting-edge books for communities of developers, administrators, and newbies alike. For more information, please visit our website: `www.packtpub.com`.

About Packt Open Source

In 2010, Packt launched two new brands, Packt Open Source and Packt Enterprise, in order to continue its focus on specialization. This book is part of the Packt Open Source brand, home to books published on software built around Open Source licences, and offering information to anybody from advanced developers to budding web designers. The Open Source brand also runs Packt's Open Source Royalty Scheme, by which Packt gives a royalty to each Open Source project about whose software a book is sold.

Writing for Packt

We welcome all inquiries from people who are interested in authoring. Book proposals should be sent to `author@packtpub.com`. If your book idea is still at an early stage and you would like to discuss it first before writing a formal book proposal, contact us; one of our commissioning editors will get in touch with you.

We're not just looking for published authors; if you have strong technical skills but no writing experience, our experienced editors can help you develop a writing career, or simply get some additional reward for your expertise.

jQuery UI Cookbook

ISBN: 978-1-78216-218-6 Paperback: 290 pages

70 recipes to create responsive and engaging user interfaces in jQuery

1. Packed with recipes showing UI developers how to get the most out of their jQuery UI widgets.
2. Solutions to real-world development issues distilled down in a reader-friendly approach.
3. Code examples written in a concise and elegant format making it easy for the reader to adapt to their own style.

Instant Kendo UI Mobile

ISBN: 978-1-84969-911-2 Paperback: 60 pages

Practical recipes to learn the Kendo UI Mobile library and its various components for building mobile applications effectively

1. Learn something new in an Instant! A short, fast, focused guide delivering immediate results.
2. Understand the various components on the Kendo UI Mobile application framework.
3. Learn to use the various widgets in the Kendo UI Mobile library that will help you build a mobile application rapidly.

16650264R00063

Printed in Great Britain
by Amazon